GREAT SALESPEOPLE AREN'T BORN, THEY'RE HIRED

The Secrets to Hiring Top Sales Professionals

Joe Miller & Patrick Longo

Edited by Patrick Longo

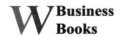

Business Books

an imprint of New Win Publishing
a division of Academic Learning Company

Copyright © 2005 by Joseph Miller
Published by WBusiness Books,
an imprint of New Win Publishing,
a division of Academic Learning Company, LLC
9682 Telstar Ave. Suite 110, El Monte, CA 91731
www.WBusinessBooks.com

Cover Design by Gary Baltazar Jr.

ISBN: 0-8329-5000-9
Library of Congress Control Number 2005920993
Manufactured in the United States of America
09 08 07 06 05   1 2 3 4 5

TABLE OF CONTENTS

Foreword V

CHAPTER 1   COMING CLEAN 1

CHAPTER 2   FILLING SOMEONE'S SHOES 11

CHAPTER 3   CREATE THE "BASE" .23

CHAPTER 4   FILL THE POOL 45

CHAPTER 5   THE PHONE SCREEN 61

CHAPTER 6   BE OBJECTIVE 71

CHAPTER 7   THE INTERVIEW 79

CHAPTER 8   THE AUDITION 97

CHAPTER 9   MAKE THE OFFER .105

CHAPTER 10   SUCCESS CONDITIONING 113

CHAPTER 11   LET'S GO SELL 119

Joe's Secrets At A Glance 125

APPENDIX 1   QUESTIONS 131

INDEX 136

Author's Foreword

As a storyteller, I love to surround myself with people who love to tell stories. Some of my best "material" has been "inspired" by other people and the brilliant stories they love to tell. I did not wake up one day and decide I wanted to write professional self-help books. In the game of sales, it seems that many of our stories aren't written down for any reason. It's more of an oral history that gets passed down from salesperson to salesperson, father to son, mother to daughter, and back into the sales world. We pick up where the last person left off.

Believe me, I don't think there is anything wrong with this. Truly, I understand that our history contains much more than a bunch of ruffled farts shooting the crap over scotch or coffee (not necessarily in that order). Or even a prolific salesperson using great fact and fiction to help uncover a customer's pain. True, honest, ethical salespeople have relayed to me some of the most meaningful stories I have ever heard, and I am sincerely grateful for that. In turn, I have come clean more often in my life because I have had good salespeople and sales managers who were there to listen. Hmm. That Holy Grail of sales: being able to listen.

In some of the next several hours of your life, I am going to ask you to do one thing: listen. I have had friends who wanted to write songs, friends who wanted to write fiction, friends who wanted to write screenplays, etc. All of those genres do a fantastic job of relaying, passing down and conveying the human story, the universal spirit in all of us, no matter what country you come from, or what kind of life you lead or have lead. Stories go beyond death. Not many of us have enough influence in our professional life to go beyond death, unless we rise to a whole new level.

I must admit that other genres can be more entertaining than the professional self-help genre, but the story you are about to hear is about life. Your life. My life. And the lives of millions of people out there just like us. This is not a story about my first love, my first heartache, or how I finally got the nerve to beat up the neighborhood bully. This is about my love for this profession and the need to help perpetuate the true notion that you must give in order to receive.

As salespeople, or people who deal with salespeople on a daily basis, we spend each working day uncovering other people's pain. We aim to help and we aim to please and, through it all, make money. Therefore, we clearly hope and aim to be rewarded for helping others. At this point, however, it's time we uncovered some of our own pain: the pain in the ass we call "hiring and firing." I'm going to ask you to turn your sensitivity meter down. I am going to become the neighborhood bully. I'm going to make fun of you until you push back and do something about your number one freaking problem: hiring and retaining great salespeople.

Like me, a friend of mine believes that you need to visualize your goal in order to reach it. You also need to write it down. This is why he has had his Academy Award speech written down and stuffed in his wallet since the third grade. In it, he has reserved a space where he thanks all of his teachers, especially the crappy ones. Why? Because he learned as much from them as he did from the good ones. He also goes on to thank all of his ex-girlfriends. And should he have the misfortune of going through a divorce before he wins his award or awards (believe me, he will win at least one), he'll probably thank his ex-wife and her attorney as well.

My Academy Award speech is this foreword. I'd like to thank everyone and everything. I'd like to thank the people who are going to publish this book. I'd like to thank the people who never considered publishing this book. I'd like to thank the prospects that turn me down every day. Most of all, I'd like to thank you for taking the verbal fanny spanking you are about to receive. And hopefully, one day you will thank me, somewhere, in a speech for being such a great inspiration… either as (a) informational saint or (b) full-of-crap schmuck. If we truly live in a true/false world, then either "a" or "b" will help you find and uncover *the truth.*

J.M.
12/5/04

CHAPTER 1
COMING CLEAN

CHAPTER 1
COMING CLEAN

When I look back on my life in sales, each chapter of my career seems as though it could be a chapter in a book. Sometimes, I even feel as though one chapter in this book could constitute its own book. However, when I approached a friend with the idea of actually writing this book, I realized that my career really came down to three phases: sales, sales training, and sales recruiting. Perhaps I felt compelled to start with sales recruiting because it is the latest chapter in a rewarding sales career and in some ways may be the most difficult phase to talk about or teach in the traditional sense. In this chapter, you will understand why.

Just as my career at this point in the game could be boiled down to three phases, so could the basic ingredients for this book. The basic ingredients of this book can be traced back to three distinct things, and represent the following: a sales recruiting manual I developed, telltale experiences I had in the sales recruiting business, and an intense desire to help other people avoid the mistakes I have made.

I am not a writer. I am a salesperson. I spend the majority of my time doing what I do, not writing it down. If I am not doing it, I am speaking about it. In the process of trying to write this down so I could share my experiences with others in a more concrete format, I realized that writing and speaking are two very different monsters. Speaking and writing (listening and reading) cater to two very different learning styles and, according to some, use different parts of the brain. So it is no shock that what I ended up with is a very colloquial, sometimes gritty style for much of this book. My goal is to speak *to* you, not *at* you.

I hope for the most part this "style" reveals my experience as a trainer, because what we learn from teaching is invaluable, and in turn makes us better teachers. Much of this book is culled from recordings I made of my training ("teaching") sessions. Hearing myself on audiotape and looking at the original transcription both intrigued and amused me, because the man I heard was different from the man I saw in my own head, and vice versa. It's important to keep this in mind while reading this book, because how you see yourself and how others see you may be two completely different things. In fact, that's a guarantee. The discrepancy might be a little and it might be almost unbearable. That's why I call this chapter "coming clean."

One of the best ways to judge yourself is to watch yourself on video. Listening to and watching one's self on video can be very humbling and, in some cases, humiliating. It also can be refreshing. You catch your mistakes, but you also catch a glimpse of your own shine. Most importantly you realize there is plenty of room to grow. And growth is always what we're looking for in life and in business. At least that's my belief, and I'm 99.44% sure it's your belief as well, or you wouldn't be caught dead paying for this book, much less taking the time to read it.

Salespeople are among the top 10% of income earners in this country, and you are charged with the task of hiring salespeople. As a side note, it's amazing to me that the people who spend money on self or professional improvement often don't need it and the people who need it don't do anything for their own improvement. Through the secrets in this book, you can improve and/or make more money. One or both will and can make you happy depending on your definition of "happy!"

How many of us have watched a great sporting event and thought, "I can do that?" It's what makes the great ones "great." They make it look so easy that they make us believe we can rise to the same heights and glory, as if these "powers" were inherent or had been granted at birth. It's an illusion. Think Houdini. Think Copperfield. They got where they were, at the height of their powers, through persistence, curiosity, and hard work. The glory came later, and at this point I am sure you are ready for the glory.

Rising to the heights of sales is not always glorious, and each person's definition of "glory" will be the main determinant to whether or not any one person sees himself or herself as happy, gratified, or successful. It's not just about the money. It's so much more. If it's just about money, then you've already lived "half a death." What you give to get money without regard for your life will take away nearly all or more than it can give.

I know we are taught to be weary of a person who says, "Trust me," but if I could, without making you weary of me in the opening paragraphs of my book, I would say, "Trust me." In fact, I'll say it, say it loud and tell you to eat it. The years in my life when I was making more money were not necessarily my happiest years. Some of those years were littered with bad judgment and bad behaviors that nearly sank me, yet these were crucial errors that helped me decide where I wanted to be in my life. They taught me who to trust, when to use my instinct, and when to use my head. They taught me as much about family as they did about business, even though I always considered myself a "family guy." There are places in life to gamble and places where you should use pure logic. I know it's logical to hire great salespeople to limit your pain. Gambles are different than risks.

I have always risked a lot, but also gambled. My past, in many ways, yielded more opportunities through setbacks (gambles) than successes. But this kind of success only comes from learning: learning through mistakes. If you do not learn, you just go further down the hole, and somewhere along the line, you can only hope to learn there's a madness that must end. One of the greatest gambles you can make is to resist change, to just sit there and think that things will magically turn for the better if you leave things as they are. Anyone who says, "If it ain't broke, don't fix it" most likely doesn't have a personal definition of "broken."

In my life, the opportunities given through risk were greater, more challenging, and more rewarding than anything else in life. Risks can be calculated and bring less pain than gambles. After watching the movie *Wall Street*, I realized that greed indeed is good to a point, but when taken to the extreme it will bite you. It's piggish and unnecessary because there is plenty to go around. Unfortunately, more often than not, greed bites the little man, the struggling person, and the person who can't recover as quickly from the consequences as someone who has a little insurance, so to speak. Greed often affects people who are not greedy. Believe me, this is not a manifesto, but a slight warning from a little guy who thinks big. I'm 5'9" but not Napoleonic.

I don't want to get too Zen on a bunch of salespeople, but in the past years I also learned how the simple act of giving can bring each one of us success in our own lives. If life is all about me, how can I expect to *get* anything in life? What do I have to compare it to? Who do I have to share it with? Everything is reciprocal, and the more honest I can be as a salesperson, the more honest I can be as a person. Remember there is a "person" in salesperson. That is why I can honestly say I would never sell a person something they truly did not need. I would never hire a person I did not need. And I would never fire a person simply because I did not "need" them. I call on myself to be responsible and find or create a job in my company that will utilize a person's skills to generate revenue.

That's why this book is not about training. Real growth is new business, not cooking the old books and calling it new stew! If you are truly hiring for talent, you can always use that person in some way, but salespeople are not necessarily professionals you would want to retrain for a different position. You may just need to find more creative ways to utilize the talent they possess for their current profession. It takes hard work, so start with the talent that you hired them for; but if it's a losing proposition, own up to it and let them go.

 Remember: in your business stew, good salespeople are the most effective ingredient.

Every person in a company has a purpose or they wouldn't be there. If they are not doing their job you can fire their ass, but only after you've given them an opportunity to change their ways. It may simply be that you screwed up and hired the wrong person. Or maybe you unconsciously hired them for another position. In either of these case scenarios, *they* should be giving *you* a chance to change your ways, or you should efficiently help them find their stride in your company. Otherwise, improve yourself or step up to the plate, take a deep breath, and fire yourself! Yes. Fire yourself. Go where your true talents are useful. There's nothing shameful in that. Come clean.

If a good salesperson is not doing well in your company, is that necessarily their fault? It may well be, but the easiest thing you could do is give up… and fire their ass! That may mean *you* are weak. Or lazy, or… Is that too harsh? If so, you may want to close the cover and take this book right back to the bookstore and ask for your money back. Make sure you tell them why you didn't like the book. Really. Is it because the language is too harsh or because the weakness starts with you? Come clean. Maybe this is a management problem, but what we are talking about here is what we refer to as a hiring problem.

Admitting weakness is one of the strongest things a person can do. Admitting weakness in your company may be admitting you're weak, a double negative for which most people do not wish to take credit. That's understandable, but if each person cannot see their own weakness, you're going to be leaving the decisions in the hands of everyone above you in the company. If you're at the top at this moment in your life and business career, you're automatically yelling "Scapegoat!" Most of us don't have the luxury. Finding a scapegoat is one of the greatest acts of weakness available to management.

It may be true that indeed one must become a great salesperson in order to learn how to hire a great salesperson, but if you truly have both the company and the salesperson's interests laid out on the table, from the beginning, you shouldn't have to be a great salesperson. You can save both parties a lot of time, energy, money, and even a little (dare I say it?) heartbreak if you simply know what you are looking for in a great salesperson.

Anyone with a wee-bit of instinct, a pure method (provided here, thank you), and the curiosity and drive of a true professional can hire great salespeople. No, you don't necessarily have to be a good salesperson, but you definitely should know one. And, of course, you should be able to communicate effectively with the people who ultimately make the hiring decisions. In this case, it should be you. If not, then you should consider using your influence to correct the mistakes of the people who have the true influence, the real decision maker in your company. That's a bold step and I thank you for it. That, too, is hard work and can be a little unnerving.

So this book really is about coming clean and committing yourself to a true process where none exists. Or changing a process that clearly does not work. Get to know yourself. Getting to know oneself is the key to knowing how to hire someone else. Getting to know yourself is the key to influencing someone else. Getting to know yourself is the key to fixing something that is broken. Getting to know yourself is the key to understanding when you have succeeded. And finally, it is the key to keeping strong and consistent in the present and the future, which should span your entire career.

As with sales, we need to uncover what's broken if we are to successfully hire the best of the best. I assume it is the *method* or *process* you use for hiring and retaining great salespeople. If you do not know who you are and what you truly want, you are going to lead good people down a wasteful, hurtful, needless path in their life. And yours! And your company's! Although later I will talk about the ability to not take things personally in sales, leading a person on in any situation in life is uncalled for because it is unnecessary if all involved are honest about their intentions.

Unfortunately, our main barrier as human beings is that most of us do not know our intentions because we rarely look inward enough to understand ourselves. It is unfortunate that this becomes a trickle-down situation. If we don't get to know ourselves, how can we know our company? Our clients? Our prospects? Or the forest for the trees? I'm not talking about depth psychology here, just a basic self-knowledge and the need for a true process that helps reveal what we truly want when we aim to hire.

Carl Jung once stated, "It is, unfortunately, only too clear that if the individual is not truly regenerated in spirit, society cannot be either, for society is the sum total of individuals in need of redemption." If we take this quote and replace "individual" with "salesperson" and "society" with "business," you can see that the individual makes a company what it is at any moment in its life cycle. This is why I highly suggest throughout this book that a company get to know what it is looking for before it decides to hire individuals, who in many ways might be there just to make a buck. A mutual, natural distrust between management and staff only fuels this attitude, and it is wasteful and needless. You might want a salesperson that is "all about the money." That's fine if that is what you want, and you have actually thought about why this personality is good for your company.

In the past, I let greed fuel some of my decisions, and it gave me nothing but the unique opportunity to learn from my mistakes. If you consider me as "lucky" for coming to this conclusion or epiphany, then I can see we have a lot of work to do. It is only lucky if you have no stake or true investment in your actions and your control over your life, which includes work. More than half our waking days consist of work and/or preparing for work. This is a very large investment, to say the least. Taking responsibility for that time will consistently open new doors. I guarantee it.

If you and your company are not likely to learn from your or its mistakes, then you need to approach this more carefully than others. Some companies cannot afford mistakes. Anheuser-Busch can afford mistakes! SONY can make mistakes. Salespeople can make mistakes, *but if you hire bad salespeople, you may be making the greatest mistake of all.* Let's make it clear:

1. With great salespeople and bad marketing, a company can still survive.
2. With good salespeople and bad marketing, a company may survive.
3. With bad salespeople and good marketing, a company will not survive.

So what makes a good salesperson? Much of that is determined by the company the salesperson works for day to day, year after year. And yes, I do mean that the manner in which you run your company can and will help determine a salesperson's success. How many salespeople do you think do not make it through the first year in a bad company? I wish I had the statistics, though I'm sure they're out there somewhere. The answer, of course, is too many!

When looking at the sales game and how we determine who makes a good salesperson, we may (see: "should" and "have to") have to look at ourselves and figure out who we are, where we are, and where we want to go. Anyone making a hiring or firing decision must be aware of the company's direction, their personal management styles, and perhaps their own personal definition of success. That is why this book became so much a part of me, because the game of sales really is about me, and you, and anyone else who has the courage to pick up a book in order to better themselves, their salespeople, and the outside salespeople that affect your slice of the worldwide business pie. And by outside, I mean your competition!

Before you read the rest of the book, I have one disclaimer. I am from the school of low-tech. You won't find Ph.D. or any other letters next to my name. The closest thing to an educational title you will see next to my name is perhaps a sentence such as, "*Joe Miller's Dv.D.* player broke in the summer of 2002 when he tripped over his daughter's dollhouse and smashed his head against a VCR in his failed attempt to switch off MTV and play *Dumbo* for his son." What you will find, however, is honest-to-goodness real-world experience, failures and successes that are all related to hiring salespeople. So now that we're one step closer to coming clean, let's get down to business by reading this book: part seminar transcript, part manual, and mostly... experience.

CHAPTER 2
FILLING SOMEONE'S SHOES

FILLING SOMEONE'S SHOES

My "artistic" friend once told me that the biggest problem in getting a script sold is that the screenwriter, in many ways, must become his or her own personal salesperson. Now, I'm going to stereotype and say that many artists don't make good salespeople and maybe most salespeople don't make very good artists. Perhaps it's just that neither takes the time or has the patience to practice and exercise the skills needed to perform in the opposite medium.

My friend explained that when pitching a script, most amateur screenwriters are told to stop starting their Hollywood pitch with, "Basically…" This is because no story is basic, and the word itself takes too much time in a town where you literally get twenty-five words or less to convey a complicated idea. Besides, it's like starting a sales pitch with a big "Umm!" It shows insecurity, passivity, or weakness, like saying "um" with your head down at the ground, arm behind your back, etc.

The natural reason so many screenwriters start their pitch with "Basically" is because a producer's time is short and the screenwriter is trying to say that their story all comes down to something simple that can attract further listening. That something is the heart or essence of the screenplay: bare bones, solid theme, and, hopefully, the answer to the producer's dreams. The producer's dreams might be their pain. If they recently had a major flop, they need a success quick or they're not likely to be making movies any longer.

The tool screenwriters (and agents, if the screenwriter is lucky enough to have one) use to communicate the essence of their script is called a *logline*. Twenty-five words or less. That's all they have, in many instances. Picture the poor screenwriter (who somehow got into an upscale Hollywood restaurant he can't afford) bumping into his favorite producer (who he actually has stalked for some time) and the producer, without being completely peeved, says, "Okay kid, what have you got?" *That*, my new friends is what we call a high-pressure sale! Developing this pitch is a very hard thing to do. So much so that some screenwriters get another person to write the logline for them and hire yet another person to coach them on how to say/present the logline in person. For the artist, writing the screenplay is almost always easier than trying to sell it. It took 16,000 words to complete, so how can it be sold in 25 words or less?

A BIT OF HISTORY

Does the screenwriter's situation sound familiar to you? Do you have someone in front of you, arms crossed, twiddling their fingers, expecting you to fix a problem? Do they want you to sum up what you're going to do to fix this problem? Are they asking you to sum it up in twenty-five words or less? How badly would you simply like to put both of your hands up in the air and say, "I got it covered"? Let's take a moment to take a look at the following scenario and see if this matches your current predicament:

Boss: We've been losing 25K in sales each quarter this year and I'm about to take out my proctology glove to find out what's rotten in here.

You: I got it covered.

Boss: Joe Schmoe calls in sick every other Tuesday when we go over our latest sales figures and he says he was assured in his interview that he was authorized to golf on the company account as part of his comp plan.

You: I got it covered.

Boss: Our competition outsold us for the fourth quarter in a row, nearly 2 to 1 and our numbers say that's going to increase again in the next quarter.

You: I got it covered.

Boss: The CEO is coming into town and wants to know who our most effective sales manager is this year because he's starting to think you *all* suck.

You: Um. Uh. Well...

Boss: I assume you got *that* covered, too?

You: (Gulp!)

It's not easy to gain enough trust for someone to take "I got it covered" for an answer. How does Joe Miller sum up what he wants to say, in order for you to trust me? How do I tell you "I got it covered"? What's *my* logline? It simply cannot be summed up in twenty-five words, and neither can your pain. I call it a book! I like high-pressure sales, but let's take our time on this one. This story starts with a guy who thought he had it "covered" and was stupid enough to say so, out loud without a hint, clue, or plan to cover his butt.

So *basically*... here begins the story. For about the last six years, I have had a successful training company, which, of course, was determined by my definition of success. I traveled all over the country, training, having a great time, and living a great lifestyle. Generally, I was targeting and working with small to mid-size sales companies and each week I had a demanding road schedule that was exhausting, but completely exhilarating.

Sometimes things stick in your mind like burnt egg on an old frying pan. With me it's mostly the moments themselves or the minute catalysts for the memories. I still remember the day I sat down with a client, and I was shooting the breeze in a serious way, explaining how there were three kinds of salespeople: Tigers, Horses and Dogs.

I told him, "You've gotta feed your tigers, whip your horses, and take your dogs out back and shoot 'em."

I think he found this amusing, which of course was good, but then he presented me with a challenge. He said, "Well, this is my problem: you see, I've got two dogs on my team and you want me to fire both of 'em, and I can't find any good ones to replace them."

It's then that I had "the moment" which I remember crystal clear to this day. If this were a film, this might be projected in slow motion, the sound of my voice hitting low on the register like a barge wreck in the mud of the great Mississippi. I opened my big fat sales mouth and said, "That's a piece of cake. I'll find them for you." Translation: "Don't worry, be happy. I got it covered." It's the easiest thing to say and the hardest thing to do and at that point, none of that mattered.

It definitely was an open mouth-insert foot situation because sure enough, the client said, "Good, then find them for me." Who was "them"? I had no idea who "them" was at this point because I had yet to discover what the hell I had said. I do know, however, that the "me" that accepted my client's challenge seemed to echo endlessly throughout the room and off into some remote part of Iowa.

I don't know if I heard much of what he said next because I was already thinking of what I should *do* next. And, as anyone knows, thinking in/during a sales call is bad. Sell now, think later. Reaction time should be immediate and seamless or you're dead. I was dying right there, though not so much of a heart attack than of an outright digestive anomaly. I think they might have heard my stomach churn in Iowa, right behind my voice's echo.

Looking back, I don't think the situation was that bad. Why couldn't I find him a couple of tigers? It's not like I had a lot of work, even if it was just about the busiest I've ever been in my life! Now I suppose these are the so-called "defining moments" of our lives, and I appropriately did what anyone would do: I opened up the Yellow Pages and found and called recruiters! Of course, that was almost as easy as saying "I got it covered."

RECRUITERS: A DOG'S BEST FRIEND

Before we go further, let me further expound on my animal analogy here: The main thing to remember is that a horse will run and win if whipped, a dog will generally rely on you to get it through its life. It aims to please but usually doesn't do much more than keep you company and look at you lovingly with those puppy eyes. Obviously, service dogs are the exception, but you get my drift. Tigers, however, are solitary. They are self-reliant. They live for the hunt and the kill and will patrol large territories to get what they need to live. They are skilled predators that always take home the prize. Who would you rather have working for you? Throughout this book, I'll further expound on this analogy, because it is easier to talk about this than it is to apply it in the field and to the trade and we need to consistently point out where it's relevant.

Now we've all heard that dogs are man's best friends, yes? In a loving kind of way, you might say that sales dogs often become a recruiter's best friends. Unfortunately, many recruiters simply feed dogs to companies. Dogs are easy: willing, seemingly able, and aiming to please. They slobber all over the recruiter. The bodies come to them and the position is filled, mainly because most people don't know how to interview, and dogs are great at getting through interviews with people who don't know what they're doing. This will be very important later on in this book.

It seems recruiters just can't find the courage to find their 12-gauge, take the dogs out back and pump 'em full of lead. Please believe me. I'm 100% dog owner, but I want my dog to be a dog and my kitty to grow up to be a cat, but *I want my salespeople to be tigers.* My reward on that day, besides the lovely taste of my size-8 wingtip (I told you I was short), was a first-class ticket to becoming a certified Head Hunter.

If you ever truly examined the process of head hunting, you'd understand that there's a unique problem that is apparent right from the beginning of this process. Even if a recruiter were well aware that they were interviewing all dogs, or even if they were qualified to spot a dog, the company's definition of success determines whether or not the recruiter succeeds. According to the flimsy definition I was putting out there, the recruiters were truly succeeding. This is because I had one definition: find me bodies. Bodies are easy to find. Any smart-ass recruiter could have brought me to a cemetery, put out their hand and said, "You know my fee."

Fast-forward to my new definition of success and you find yourself reading my book. My new definition is to find the best salespeople who are best suited for the company for which they apply, based on the company's rock-solid definition. It's true that I often help them define the perfect salesperson, but nonetheless we will not move forward until this definition is in place. If not, the process immediately can be deemed useless.

I feel as though I am genuinely certified now, because clients have paid me thousands to find them tigers, based on their rock-solid definition of a tiger. If I do not live up to this agreement, they can ask for their money back or I must try again. If they are specifically paying me to find them dogs, however, then I am successful when I find them a dog. And I can sleep at night.

The only problem is this: just about *any* recruiter out there is qualified to find you dogs. Take the highway to work and look for the guy with his head out his window. Look for the guy marking the trees in the park.

Turn back the clock and you'll remember that this initial client wanted a tiger, and seeing there was no manual and time was not on my side, I took the job and felt quite pleased to know I was a self-certified Head Hunter. The client instantaneously certified me and was going to pay me for my first recruiting job.

I definitely felt qualified to search the Yellow Pages. Who wouldn't? We've been trained to do that since the fourth grade. Unfortunately, every other step in this process I would have to make up as we went along. Does this sound familiar? Does your body language say, "I got it covered," when your heart is saying, "My God, I don't want to go through this crap again. Why can't these salespeople just do their job, make lots of money, stay here forever on a crappy comp plan and like me for who I am?" I wouldn't be kidding if I told you that you are not alone on this cruel planet.

THE GAMBLE THAT HUMBLED

I was now on another great professional adventure and at the start of an entirely new career. I proceeded to look up every recruiter, and do business with each one that would return my phone call. If they didn't return my call, I quietly slipped back into my salesperson's shoes and got them to call me or take my call. Soon enough, it was hard to determine who was selling whom. Sure enough, I got what one might call the typical recruiter's "M.O." They came to me and asked me many brilliant questions. It all sounded reasonable as it left the recruiter's lips. Who did I want to hire? What did I want to hire? When did I want to hire? Where did I want to look for this hire? How much do I want to pay this hire?

I got to work right away, writing the job description, the compensation plan, the ad for the paper... everything! More than proud of myself, I chose what seemed to be the most qualified recruiter and submitted all of my research and information. He called me a few days later and said, "Great! We'll find you someone soon." Most animals have a heightened sense of smell, and at this point, whether I was a tiger or a dog, I should have smelled the dogs coming. Maybe I just marked my territory as a dog and not a tiger. Maybe I forgot to take my head out of the car window.

Anyone who's even vaguely familiar with the recruitment process knows the terror when the process actually begins. The recruiter came through, as promised, and my fax machine would never be the same. Yes, he started sending me résumés. I got flooded with résumés. I was afraid to light a match for fear of starting a genuine forest fire or a big time flourmill explosion, but I had to look through every single one of them. Reading them was the least of it. I actually read them, planned the interviews, called people in, and spent my time with these people until I was comfortable choosing three or four people I thought were good. Real tigers, all of them.

Feeling as though I could finally stretch my feet out and crack my knuckles, I sent the three or four good candidates to my client and paid the recruiter his share. Ninety days later, my client called up a little less than wonderfully satisfied (perhaps truly pissed off). Out of the three candidates that they hired, one quit, one got fired, and one couldn't sell anything to save his life. Yep, they sucked. While I had an angry client jumping down my throat and up my ass seemingly at the same time, the recruiter in all likelihood found himself sipping Italian wine (paid for by my sweat) under the Tuscan sun.

The great thing to remember here is this: the recruiter was successful based on my definition of success *for him.* Conversely, I was highly unsuccessful based on my own limited definition of success. I was supposed to provide tigers and instead gave the candidate a couple of dogs and a tired old horse. At this point, all I had was a picturesque but flimsy animal analogy with no way of determining its actual meaning in the real sales world.

Out of all my failures, this ranks up there by the Jolly Green Giant's nose hairs. I truly got egg on my face because the recruiter got all the money and the client was pissed off... at me! Seeing that bad moments serve as positive reminders that something has to change, I sat down and, like Socrates before me, said, "There's got to be a better way." In fact there must be a *much* better way to hire salespeople. One of the reasons this sticks out in my mind is because I had to get back on the horn and do what I do best... sell! In order to learn, improve, and succeed in this new venture, I simply had to do some research and selling of my own. I had to uncover people's pain, find a solution that works and sell it. At this point, I was already backlogged with a mad customer who had already given me two referrals. There was no way I was going to fail twice. This was a *gamble* that turned into failure and I needed to *learn* so that it paid off. Once I had an actual *process*, I would *risk* everything to turn it into a business. This comes later.

THE PROCESS OF FINDING A PROCESS

Armed with a good dose of humiliation turned determination, I called dozens of recruiters all over the country and realized that all recruiters are the same. If you haven't noticed, I'm not necessarily knocking them, because the industry has accommodated certain behaviors, and anyone who wants to go beyond and above the current call of duty could actually get some solid work done.

I still remember one particular day in Cleveland, Ohio, where I was meeting with a new, hotshot recruiter. I truly respected this guy, so I was pushing him pretty hard, to the point where I had him up against the wall. He had his share and finally put his hands up and said, "C'mon, Miller. I didn't meet with you to overhaul an industry. What is it that you really want?" I didn't realize the tirade I had been on and finally relaxed. This was my chance, so I did what came natural to me. I opened my big fat mouth once again and blurted:

QUOTES

"Here's what I want. I want you to come to my company and tell me what kind of salesperson I am. I want you to look at my sales team, look at my management practices and tactics, and I definitely want you to look at my competition. And when you're done with that, tell me if my comp plan is too high, too low… what's going on? Do I have the right model? The wrong model? I want you to define the perfect salesperson and, when you've defined it, I want you to find him or her. And I don't want you to look in some database of people who are 'supposed' to be good. I want you to find me someone you never met before. I want you to interview them. I want you to test them and I want you to interview them again and again. I want you to beat the living daylights out of them until you think they're perfect. Then I want you to ship them to me, and I want to hire them. I want to have one interview and hire the guy. And then I want them to go out and I want them to be perfect and I want you to take full responsibility for their success or failure. And if it doesn't work, I want you to find me another one."

JUNGLE FEVER

When I was done panting, I wiped the foam out of the corners of my mouth and retracted my claws back into my paw pads. I still remember how the recruiter sort of sat back, scratched his chin, chuckled, and then began to laugh at me outright. It certainly broke the tension that had built up in the room, but I still didn't know where his laughter was taking this. He finally relaxed, looked at me for a brief moment without a word, and said, "Miller, when you find that, I'll come work for you." Those words have fueled me and driven me harder more than any other feedback, suggestions or challenges I have received throughout the long, hard, learning process that I call my life. As you may guess, that was the beginning of our company, *SalesKingdom*.

SalesKingdom arose from a basic, simple, unfulfilled need that was not being met, according to this new definition. Unfortunately, the solution seems simple and actually can be quite complicated and hard to duplicate, *especially if it is not written down.* We quickly realized that we wanted the same thing that everyone else wanted but couldn't find. This was one hell of an itch that needed a scratch. This required a whole different breed of recruiters that did not exist, and if they did, then they might as well have been in the Congo somewhere in some remote jungle with all the other fabled beasts that exist but have eluded human contact for years. And I was too tired to wield a machete!

That was 1998, and SalesKingdom was conceived and implemented. We decided our company should solely be "dedicated to the advancement of the sales professional," which is our motto to this day. Our mission at SalesKingdom is to help salespeople improve their careers and find better jobs in order to help companies who are looking for perfect salespeople. We help companies find their match through a distinct process that you will learn here.

Since then, we have gained tremendous amounts of experience, learned a lot of hard-won lessons, and created a process to hire better salespeople. This book is all about the process I simultaneously developed and learned as the Head Hunter for SalesKingdom, and it's a process I have written down so you too may recruit the best and brightest salespeople for your company.

Now that you understand how I forced myself to fill someone else's shoes, perhaps we both have "come clean." I was in your shoes for a long time and I still am, every working day and even in my dreams and nightmares. I forced myself into this situation because I opened my mouth and took the ball to the court, just like you have. And, I continued forward because I love and respect this profession and live to help uncover people's pain. I don't expect us to agree on everything, but hopefully we both can agree that you will not be able to start any new process without a "base," especially the process you are about to learn.

Before we continue, I want to make it clear that the process we are about to discuss is an overview of an extremely detailed procedural recruiting manual at my company, SalesKingdom. At any one point in the process, SalesKingdom has a highly qualified researcher, recruiter, account manager and salesperson to initiate and carry out this process. I don't expect any company to have the resources to emulate that, and suggest you use all of your available resources and creativity to match certain procedural tasks with the skills and talent you have, currently. Therefore, this book is more of a process guide for the reader.

I have found that the process works, always, but it is only as good as your commitment to following what's there. Its parts can continually be adjusted, not in how they are ordered or what tasks need to be completed, but how they are to be completed. One quick example is the employment ad. The process dictates you will be placing an ad, somewhere, at a specific point. However, the process cannot guarantee you write a good ad, that you place the ad in the right places, nor if you are paying too much or too little for the ad. That says nothing about the process, just how you commit one task within the process. If you hold up the integrity of the process and readjust what doesn't work due to your own learning curve, it will undoubtedly bring results. This book is your guide.

CHAPTER 3
CREATE THE "BASE"

CREATE THE "BASE"

Whenwe set about building a process for finding great salespeople, we knew our first order of business was to create a system that could be explained, taught, and repeated. Like most men, we love acronyms and will gladly create one just for the hell of it. If it actually fits and makes sense, then it is all the better! Somehow it makes you feel like some sharp, smarmy NASA engineer creating a language that regular beer-drinking, football-watching men might not understand no matter how many times he watches the Discovery or History channels. Knowing acronyms is like being part of that special club. All joking aside, this particular acronym makes simple sense. In everything we build, make, create or teach, from erecting buildings to cooking from recipes, we have to start with a solid *base*.

LEARN FROM YOUR MISTAKES

The biggest mistake people make when trying to identify the perfect salesperson is their failure to figure out what they're looking for, first. This is not like a first date, where you're going to get swept off your feet and declare your love for a person without really knowing them that well. You should be wiser now, acting more mature, and hopefully you have played the field a little bit. You understand that people are not always who you think they are, and that instant love is blinding, too trusting, and too accepting. Most of all, *you should be confident that you know what you want.*

Did you ever know anyone who "got married too soon"? You know, the people who have bridesmaids and groomsmen who can barely keep their lips shut as the priest asks, "Does anyone object to this union? Speak now or forever hold your peace." Finding the perfect salesperson is like finding the perfect husband or wife. I want to personally save you from a bitter divorce from someone you thought was perfect. This is the time to speak now, or forever hold your peace. We know things are screwed and will continue to be so if we do not seek pre-marriage counseling or seek to find a better mate.

After reading this book you should feel like you got your "second chance" to do it right, knowing now what you should have known before you ended up in a divorce situation. This generally means you have one, many, or all of the following problems/issues:

1. Poor employee retention
2. Poor employee performance
3. Managerial lack of vision
4. Lack of guidance
5. Comp plan equity issues
6. Rogue/Unmanageable employees
7. Poor morale
8. Poor company performance
9. Lack of measurable employee milestones

Any one of these issues can lead to a "divorce" situation, which includes, but is not limited to the following:

1. Someone is leaving the company.
2. Someone is fired.
3. Someone is being "harassed" or made to feel uncomfortable so they "quit."
4. Someone is causing serious morale issues.
5. There are fractured loyalties in different departments.
6. There's fractured loyalty in one department.
7. Someone decides not to take a job with your company.

I'LL BE SEEING YOU, IN ALL THE SENTIMENTAL PLACES

I agree that it's great to look at your past and learn from your mistakes, but too many employers don't think of the simple changes that can be made to do things better. Some of the changes you need to make might not be that drastic. When hiring, most managers will look at their existing sales team or at their hiring history, bad or good, and go headstrong into a negative situation that seems to go on, ad infinitum. Someone leaves or is fired from the company, and someone from management comes in and says:

"Well, let's just submit the old ad to the Daily Rhubarb, describe the position, and let's be ready to go. Let 'em ride for a week with Big Bill in Department Z and have them learn the ropes. And, uh, make sure they only get one drink ticket to this year's holiday party. They won't be here six months yet before then and, uh, we got the retirees coming this year and they can't get enough of the eggnog. Besides, they gotta prove themselves just like I did after I came back from the war. Give 'em that old chair that hurts their ass. That'll keep 'em alert... toughen 'em up. Hell, that was here since the other war when old Jonesy was still here."

Every time you hire someone new you are given the chance to do things right, or to actually make a change.

Do these employers really believe they have learned from their mistakes? That's definitely the wrong way to approach the hiring scenario. Would you look at an ex-lover, ask them out again and be fine with the way things were, even though you know you were a poor fit the first time around? In general, people don't change and if a faulty process doesn't change, you're not going to have any better luck finding a successful hire than you would a fifth go at it with your ex-lover. Don't you know you could find someone better? Or do you think that you're probably better off staying single and waiting for the right one to come along?

Waiting is better than screwing it up. Looking for a lousy salesperson through the same lousy process is like taking back an ex-lover from a bad relationship merely to fill the hole in your life. Unlike lousy dates, salespeople aren't there to accompany you through the otherwise lonely holiday season, only to be dumped after New Year's Day. They're not there long enough to escort you to your mother's third cousin's wedding. They are there to fill a hole in a positive way, and they are there to make you money.

Why ask the same person out on a date again, when you know it didn't work the first time? Are you trying to sabotage yourself and your company? Don't get sentimental about how things are or were.

If you want a candlelight dinner reunion with your ugly past, then fine. Stop reading. If I were the government, I would beg congress to institute a law that would tax you for such behavior and invest it in people who have moved on. You have to look at what the perfect salesperson *should* be doing, now. I'm not saying you can't be emotional or use your instinct now and then because that's the subject for yet another book. Instincts are good. Sentimentality is bad.

However, you might not need more logic here either, because you're prob-ably being *too* logical. The truth of the matter is that you just need to stop being apathetic, lazy, or slothful. Again, waiting is better than screwing it up, but from now on, you are going to be proactive and confident that you can find the right date and have a happy marriage in your company because the right people are going to come to you. If they're not right, you're going to know it and you're going to say, "no, thanks!" Most of all, you will stop fearing *change*.

BASE: THE PERFECT INGREDIENTS

When building our new process, we simply looked toward the basic things we were using to hire salespeople, besides instincts and logic. These "basic things" lead us to our new principle, which gave us our excuse to come up with our one and only acronym, aptly named BASE. BASE stands for:

1. Behaviors
2. Attitudes
3. Skills Sets
4. Environment

When my editor read this book for the first time he let me know that I refer to BASE so much that he almost got sick of seeing it. In reality, however, I still can't say enough about it because this process is nothing without it. It's the driving force of the process and, therefore, this book. I can let you get sick of the acronym, but never the process. You might learn to hate the life raft, but it's the best or only thing that's going to get you to shore. After that, you can play with the siren in the ambulance, but that's just another vehicle that's going to lead you to the hospital, where we're taking you to deal with your pain. First, let's look at your life raft: Behaviors, Attitudes, Skills Sets and Environment.

BEHAVIORS

In sales, we constantly should be looking at the specific behaviors that drive our sales tactics. We need to go further than we think: look at behaviors required for the salesperson to sell to the client. We also need to look at the typical behaviors for the client or prospect as well. Think verb or action. You want a proactive salesperson first, a reactive salesperson second.

Think of what the perfect salesperson *should* be doing, not what your current salespeople *are* doing. If you don't, you're still living in the past trying to date your ex-lover, and a good friend, family member, priest or colleague should slap you a couple of times, tell you to stop crying, and move on. In this case, that person will be me.

At this point, there are no more excuses. You simply did things wrong in the past, as most people do, and now you're going to correct it because you are going to take your time, confident that you have a system in place to direct you and steer you away from past mistakes. In changing your business behaviors, you will be better equipped to understand sales behaviors.

Sales behaviors are actions like cold-calling, prospecting, networking, how you *typically* generate sales for your business, or, more importantly, how you *want* to generate sales for your business. For those of you who hire salespeople but aren't in sales, let's do a quick review, because I get the sense at this point that I may be using terms that have different meanings for different people, so let's go over some definitions first.

There are four basic activities you can do in the world of prospecting. The first is called *cold-calling.* Cold-calling is when you know absolutely nothing about your prospect and they know nothing about you. There is little chance of winning this game. I did not say "no chance," just *little* chance. Many salespeople avoid cold-calling like the plague for this reason, and for many other intricate reasons that I will address in my next book. Yes, it takes that long to discuss.

The second prospecting activity is called *chasing a lead.* This is where most salespeople spend their time. This is slightly better than cold-calling. Typically, people will tell me that they cold-call when in fact they are *chasing a lead.* A lead is a person or a company that you know *should* need what you sell and *should* have the money to pay you. They know nothing about you, however, and it is your job to help them understand that they *do* need you. When cold-calling, you're not really sure of anything.

The third is called a *referral*. Read carefully the definition of a referral. A referral is a prospect that knows about you from a respected third party, *has* a need for your product, service or solution, *has* the money to pay you, is *expecting* your call, and is *ready* to talk to you when you *do* call. If the person is not expecting your call, you don't know for sure that they have a need for you and your product, service or solution. If you're not sure that they have the money to pay you, then it is just a *lead*. It's a good lead, but still a lead.

The fourth is an *introduction*. An introduction is simply a referral that is done in person. You and the prospect are invited to lunch by a third party and that third party introduces both of you and advises the prospect that they need to do business with you. To me, this is one of the easiest sales to close, but other salespeople may completely disagree. If you have hired a salesperson that can't close an introduction, get your work pants on, run to the airport, and jump on a plane heading to Iowa, because you just bought the farm… in a sorry state of affairs.

Remember that your business may depend on completely different behaviors for each of these activities and different salespeople have different ways of doing business with clients. If your business is highly focused on *new* prospecting, then cold-calling is going to have to be one of the more focused behaviors that are going to drive your sales. This shows you that you are going to have to find a salesperson that is already displaying the skills necessary, or part of the behaviors *necessary* for cold-calling potential clients.

If your business is done basically by knowing other people, and/or through referrals, then you have to find a salesperson whose behaviors are already focused on growing the business in this manner. If your business has a model where your salesperson is out in the field on appointments two times a week, two appointments a day, or two appointments a month, then those behaviors are necessary for that business model.

 What I recommend, based on what we would do in your situation, is that you find the necessary behaviors and then work backwards.

Always work backwards from the point of sale to the beginning of the sales process, whatever that may be for your company. Let me give you an example: let's say a good salesperson in your business should make one good sale a week. That's fine, but now you need to back up from there. What happens, backwards, from the sale to the first little spark that initiated the process that becomes the sale itself? If you make one sale a week, you have to ask yourself what happens before the sale or how many other transactions need to transpire before that sale can be made.

I've seen sales where a salesperson cold-calls a company, gets a credit card number, and sends the customer a receipt via e-mail within a fifteen-minute transaction. However, that's not normal! I call that telemarketing. Typically, before you can make a sale, you have to make a proposal. Think: how many proposals do you have to make in order to get one sale? Maybe the average is three proposals to get one sale. Great. But what has to happen before you can make a proposal? You have to have a meeting. If on average you have to have three meetings to get one proposal, then to get three proposals you need to get nine meetings. Now you know that you need nine meetings every week.

The law of probability says if you have nine meetings, someone is definitely going to cancel. So let's say for the sake of this example, you need ten meetings. That's two a day. In order to get two a day, how many people do you need to get in contact with to get them to agree to meet with you? Maybe you have to reach twenty people. Or, how many times do you have to *attempt* to make contact with someone because you use e-mail (which is never real-time) or reach their voice mail and they call you back when you're at lunch? "Phone Tag, you're it!"

I hope you realize that you simply have to focus on your typical sales, get to the point and build a model. When you work it backwards, one sale is three proposals, three proposals translates into ten meetings, ten meetings means twenty contacts, twenty contacts means forty attempts. You now have to find a salesperson that already makes forty attempts a week to get one sale!

If you find a salesperson that hasn't run ten meetings a week over the last ten years, what makes you think they're going to start now? You probably already have a couple of dogs on your team that you need to shoot, and now you're going to hire another one *and* try to teach them all new tricks? You sick, twisted son-of-a-bitch, you *are* trying to sabotage yourself and your company. All because you fear change? Behaviors are absolutely crucial to finding the BASE and creating the model of the perfect salesperson that can meet your needs.

ATTITUDES

The next BASE component is *attitudes*. When most people talk about attitudes, they are thinking in terms of positive, negative, cynical, optimistic, etc. That's not what we're looking for here. We only want to know the salesperson's attitudes regarding certain key elements of the sales process, and one of those key elements is going to be the exchange of money. In sales, you need to discuss it and ask for it and it's never simple because of who we are and how we grew up. What money attitudes do your salespeople need to have in order to sell to your clients and prospects. Don't stereotype here, not all salespeople are in it for the money. This is one of the dangers of assuming that greed fuels people's actions. Yes, it fuels *some* people's actions, or merely some actions of some people. Get that?

ATTITUDES: "MONEY"

Certainly, sales is a money-driven business no matter how you look at it, but the amount of money exchanged and the method we use to exchange it can be as different as chickens and bears. They both make cute stuffed animals, but the similarity ends there. Money attitudes are as complicated as the sales process itself. You have to look at how intensely your sales process focuses on money. Are you selling big-ticket items or small-ticket items? Is your typical sale 20K, 50K, 100K or is it $10.50? Determine what money attitudes you will require from your perfect candidate, including but not limited to *how* the money is exchanged and *how fast* it needs to be exchanged. Specifically, how will this determine whether or not that salesperson, and therefore the company, will be considered successful?

A typical salesperson will get their belief system from the people who raised them and their money attitude will be no different. I can still remember the lessons I got from my father regarding money. One summer, at the family Fourth of July picnic, I asked my neighbor how much he paid for the new Corvette in his driveway. With lightening speed my dad smacked me upside the head, knocking my hot dog right out of its bun and onto the ground. I didn't have time to exercise the all-powerful (and disgusting, now that I'm a parent) 10-second rule because he then proceeded to lecture me that it was rude to ask someone how much money they spent to purchase something. He went even further as to instruct me that money is the root of all evil, is a private matter, and is not to be discussed openly. I was so embarrassed I never forgot that lesson. Twelve years later I find myself in a sales position and I have to ask a person, "How much are you currently spending for your legal services?" or "What budget do you have set aside to fix the problem?" Talk about anxiety. And remember, I'm a so-called family man.

The key to making sure you have the right BASE is to make sure you know what attitudes your ideal candidate must have with money. If your perfect candidate needs to be able to sell 250K ticket items, then he should be able to talk about how it will affect the company's bottom line and profitability or how it's going to affect the CEO's personal profitability. The candidate should have very strong attitudes *about* money, should be very comfortable *talking* about money, and most importantly, they should have no problem legally taking it or receiving it. Otherwise, that salesperson will be useless.

In contrast, if you have a company generating small sales, say $150 per sale, and each sale is not really affecting the company's bottom line, top line, or anyone's personal income, then maybe your perfect salesperson doesn't need to be comfortable talking about money. You may realize that this will not be an issue for your sales process, but it is no less a key issue in finding the attitudes that you will need to uncover. Of course, we all understand that five cents can affect the bottom line when multiplied, but that should be determined by management before hiring any salespeople who may *affect* that bottom line. Know the salesperson's role in your definition of success, and you will succeed.

ATTITUDES: DECISION MAKING

Another attitude you need to uncover is how your perfect salesperson should make decisions. If your typical sales cycle is six, nine, or twelve months long and you know decisions are not made quickly, this may not be considered high-pressure sales. If there's a lot of shopping around, or basically there's a lot of comparison-shopping, then it's okay if your perfect candidate thinks that way. The same is fine with a sale that takes a lot of analysis, or a second, third or fourth meeting to complete. However, if you want this to be about the fast sale, with a quick, loosely planned transaction, then your perfect candidate has to be able to have that same decision-making process ingrained in them. That's their decision-making process "attitude," if you will. It's their mindset regarding decisions and it's very important.

Let's say you want/expect your clients and prospects to make the decision to buy on the spot from you and in their personal life, the salesperson that you hire would never make a decision to buy on the spot. Where's the logic in hiring such a person? The salesperson you hire would think it over, shop around, look for a lower price, and look for a better deal. If that's what the salesperson's internal decision-making process is like, then there's no way they're going to get your client to decide quickly. You better have a salesperson that has the same decision-making attitudes that you want your client or prospect to have. Otherwise, you'll be stuck in the Mississippi mud, waiting for your salesperson to let someone shop around while your revenue slips down the river on a riverboat.

ATTITUDES: NEED FOR APPROVAL

The third attitude is what we call the *need for approval*. The need for approval has been around for at least as long as humankind could document such things. It's probably safe to say that, with an overblown media, our increasing infatuation with fame and stardom (RealityTV?), and 24-hour coverage of everything human and inhumane, it is a much greater issue now than ever before. It seems you can't take a piss without feeling like you're being judged. "Hey! Bob. Nice angle there, but your arc is a little off when you wear your hushpuppies. Too much splatter in the later half. Try wearing your wingtips for more accuracy! Keeps your stance grounded."

We increasingly define ourselves by what other people think of our looks, our cars, our jobs, our husbands or wives, whatever. The need for approval comes from the way a person is raised in society and the way society, in effect, raises us. Jung's quote is the gift that keeps on giving. Like the proverbial onion, it has many layers. Society needs us to be individuals, but it's hard when society doesn't *want* you to be one. Without getting too touchy-feely here, it is okay to be an individual, and you will never know what makes you an individual unless you examine yourself from both a personal and business perspective. If you're truly okay with yourself, you won't really care what people think about you and you won't feel hurt when a prospect thinks you're lower than a catfish, scum-sucking bottom-feeder in hell.

This all goes back to the dog analogy I used in the beginning of the book. The main thing to remember, again, is that a horse will run and win if whipped, and a dog will generally rely on you to get it through its life. It aims to please but usually doesn't do much more than keep you company and look at you lovingly with those puppy eyes. Obviously, service dogs are the exception, but you get my drift. Tigers, however, are solitary. They are self-reliant. They live for the hunt and the kill and will patrol large territories to get what they need to live. They are skilled predators that always take home the prize. They're too focused to care what anyone thinks or feels about them. And, there's nothing unethical about the way a Tiger feeds. It's the law of the land.

Some people, many of which are hard-core cat people, don't like dogs simply because they mistake a dog's loyalty for stupidity. That uncommon loyalty can be said to be stupidity or a compete lack of self-sufficiency. The fact is that we bred and domesticated dogs to *need* us. Both salespeople and management can be accused of being dogs. The sales dogs are bred to need their managers and their managers love to look into their puppy eyes, pet them, scratch them, feed them, and send them to the doghouse for doing bad things. Then they whimper and give us the sad eyes and we repeat the process, ad infinitum. The sales dog needs to have approval from prospects, clients, and management. And once they walk out your door after work, God knows how many other people they will seek for approval.

People in management fall for this too often, because they have similar dog traits. First, they'll make the mistake of *wanting* their employees to like them. That's natural, because most of us want people to like us. You either lack the need for approval or you don't. If you don't, you need to train yourself to cut the crap. What's worse, however, is that they'll also *try* to get their employees to like them. Management needs the dog to make its numbers, so they in turn meet their numbers, and their boss's boss makes their numbers and the CEO can go off on another golf outing, dreaming of all the seminars he's going to send you to so you can make him/her more money.

You know the drill. Too many manager dogs roll over any time another dog comes strolling by, sniffing around. The problem is that they don't like the conflict. They don't like change. They don't like work: the thought of going through the dreaded process of finding someone new and training them. And nobody wants to kick a dog, especially when it's down, so the simple thing is to never hire one! Hire the right person and you won't have to train them. Hire the right person, and you won't have to kick a dog. And you won't have to work so hard. And you will all make money, right up to the Big Cheese!

If you *aren't* a management dog, I apologize for the wasted paragraphs. And, if you *are* a dog and want to keep your job, start taking classes or reading books (like this one) that help you become a (at least) horse or a tiger.

QUOTES Hunt for good salespeople like the tiger would hunt for food, and you will never have to worry about getting whipped (micromanaged) or kicked (harassed so you quit without your company having to give you unemployment, i.e., fired!).

ATTITUDES: GETTING TO KNOW YOU

In psychology, Carl Jung developed the concept of the *human shadow*. Anyone who has walked in the sun, or any light, knows that our bodies cast a shadow behind us. Jung states that the shadow can represent the qualities we hide from the world, the negative or undesirable parts of ourselves that we don't want to be seen. As we get older, the shadow grows as parents, teachers, priests, peers, government, media, etc., begin to affect and determine what we see as "desirable." This directly determines how we see ourselves and therefore determines our self-worth in society at large. By the time we get into our teens, we have a tough enough time getting onto the dance floor, much less cold-calling hundreds of people we don't know, asking them to purchase something they don't even know they need... yet.

This may explain how out of nowhere, at a cocktail party actually, a friend of mine gave me a sneering look and asked, "How do you do it?" Caught off guard, I responded with the brilliant, "Do what?" Because I knew him so well, I soon realized he was trying to determine how I could be a salesperson. After questioning him and prodding him like the salesperson I am, I immediately realized how the rejection, or better yet the fear of rejection, made him physically ill. Right there at a cocktail party, the sight of me turned his stomach, his fear of rejection manifesting itself for all to see.

Pretty powerful stuff, yes?

At this point, I felt as though I could see my friend's shadow right there in front of me, though I know it wasn't created by a lamp or by the sun. He saw the salesperson in himself as undesirable and it was clear that long ago he placed this part of himself in his shadow because he saw it as negative or undesirable. At this point, I thought words like "swarthy" and "smarmy" would come popping out of his mouth. Maybe now he wanted it back, but the fear of rejection still made him ill. That is why we sometimes find opposites attractive, because we often envy the part of us that we put away as we witness its strength in others.

This shook me a little bit, I might add, but I could only move on and explain to him that once I learned that it was only business, I was never bothered by the rejection. The failure to make a sale said no more about me than my choice of car. I'm not going to sit down and cry if my prospect doesn't like my microwave oven no more than my haircut. If a prospect says "no," it doesn't even mean the prospect or client didn't like me. It just means I have to find a way to be more successful at *doing* business. It seems that much more silly to me that management might actually want a *potential hire* to like *them*. They can like you once they work for you. We'll get back to that later.

Salespeople often want approval from their prospects. We'll teach you how to test for that, but most importantly, at this stage of the process you have to determine what your perfect salesperson's acceptable need for approval level is going to be. If you want a salesperson that is direct, aggressive, and willing to ask the hard questions, they have to have a very low need for approval. Be sure to identify this very early on in the process. You have to identify their attitudes towards rejection and gauge how high or low that fear affects that person. How important is it to you whether or not they fear or are immune to rejection? If this is sales where they're more likely to get more "no's" than "yes's," then they have to be totally immune to the fear of rejection. If they're guaranteed to receive a "no" every six months, and only every six months, then that fear is not that important.

ATTITUDES: EMOTIONAL DISCIPLINE

You also have to look at the attitude you have toward emotional discipline. Do they need to be even-keeled? Do you have a very complicated, long, drawn-out sales cycle? If so, they have to be emotionally tough. Is this a short, in-and-out cycle where the process is practically over before it begins? If so, then they don't need to be that emotionally tough because they're going to move on to the next one too quick to care much either way. You have to look at the attitude of self-discipline. If this is a process with a lot of follow-up, a lot of contact, and a lot of detail, then you have to look at that attitude and *create* that attitude by finding a salesperson to *match* that attitude.

ATTITUDES: GOAL SETTING

Another important attitude you need to look at is *goal setting*. Once again, the more complex your cycle is, the more important it is to set goals. You have to understand how important it is to have goal setting as a proper attitude. If a person is firing away and making a quick sale, your goals may be more short-term and involve less patience. If your salespeople are looking at a long, drawn-out sales process, then perhaps you may want to hire someone who can stick it out because they understand the long-term goal may be to make one or two sales. If that's your bottom line, fine. Some people are motivated strictly by numbers, and 2 may seem like a failure while 100 seems successful. If you're selling 2 MRI machines a year, you might be considered a great salesperson, while 2 cars a year is beyond dog territory.

When thinking of goal setting, look at the production and profit goals of Japan vs. that of the U.S. Monthly and quarterly profits often rule our production and profit goals, whereas Japan often looks to quality, which in turn brings loyal customers and raises production and profit over a decade! Right now, you can bet that SONY and Honda are betting serious R&D hours and spending on emerging or future technologies; real technologies, not just some flashy idea you saw in Disney's EPCOT center when you were ten. Americans are doing the same, but the goal structure is different due to the bottom line, or the definition of success.

SKILLS SETS

Once you've looked at behaviors and attitudes, again working backwards, you need to look at *skills sets*, the next ingredient in your BASE. You have to create a list of skills sets that are important in the perfect salesperson. Skills sets include the ability to set and make appointments, get past gatekeepers, get decisions made, cold-call, create proposals, and close the sale. You need to decide if you want a hunter, a farmer, or a fisherman. A fisherman waits for a fish to come to him and has the skill to yank it out of the water. A farmer mainly harvests what's there, always thinking of a better way to yield more from what he has, and a hunter seeks it out in an ever changing, and widening territory.

What skills sets are important? Skills sets are something I intend on elaborating on in my next book. These are things that can be learned, practiced and preached. Yes, it helps to have a decent personality, but that can only take you so far. You can watch skills sets *in action*. Wait until we talk about different forms and styles of interviews in later chapters and you'll understand that an interview is a sale for both the interviewer and potential hire. If you don't know what skills sets your perfect salesperson should have, then you're going to be sold, and sold good. You will be sold up the river, with a crappy bill of goods, and by a salesperson! Our process can help you ensure you don't get sold, and instead let you "sell the seller."

SKILLS SETS CHECKLIST ☑

The following skills list is provided for you to refer to and/or for you to use when you are ready to build your own BASE mode.

Will try to close	☐	Takes responsibility for results	☐
Holds tight on margins	☐	Prospects consistently	☐
Able to talk about money	☐	Recovers from rejection	☐
Can maintain emotional control	☐	Strong desire	☐
Strong bonding and rapport skills	☐	Gets to the budget	☐
Does not assume	☐	Very motivated to earn more money	☐
Effective time management	☐	Is a prospecting animal	☐
Likes to sell	☐	Won't accept put-offs	☐
Gets appointments easily	☐	Won't make inappropriate quotes	☐
Gets past the gatekeeper	☐	Has written, personal goals	☐
Gets people to make a decision	☐	Has a plan to achieve goals	☐
Good at getting referrals	☐	Has a tracking system	☐
Can get to the decision maker	☐	Knows how to handle shoppers	☐
Strong self-confidence	☐	Good listening skills	☐
No need for approval	☐	Good questioning skills	☐
Is decisive	☐	Takes control of the meeting	☐
Good at follow-up	☐	Calls at the top	☐
Knows how to read people	☐	Asks for the business	☐
Unconditional commitment	☐	Good time and organizational ability	☐
Finds out how and why people buy	☐		

When you develop the skills sets part of the BASE, make a list of the top twenty-five most important skills sets that they need to have. If they have the top twenty-five that you are looking for, look no further. Don't make the mistake of looking for more than you need, though I will focus as much or more attention on making the mistake of looking for too little.

ENVIRONMENT

Lastly, you have to look at the *environment* of your own company, the last but not least important ingredient in your BASE. Your company environment is crucial to finding the right salesperson. A 100-year-old, family run business that has very solid, detailed procedures and policies and is pretty slow in growth is an entirely different environment than that of a brand new, fresh start-up company that doesn't even have a company manual.

I've seen companies that have a corporate manual eighty-five pages long and I've seen companies that don't even know how to spell "corporate manual"! In general, I'd say a company with a manual is going to be tighter than a company that lacks one. You have to make sure you truly understand your own business environment. If you can't pin it down, find someone who can. Is it tightly managed? Look at your sales management picture. If your sales management picture is tightly managed, that's an entirely different world than one that is loosely managed.

Let me give you an example of how this comes into play. Let's say you are a new, fresh, start-up company. You are the owner, the CEO, the CFO, and the sales manager, all in one! You put on your sales manager hat and meet with the sales team once a month, ask them what they're doing and call it a day. That's about it. The company is loosely managed because you really aren't in the trenches with them, watching their every move, yet the environment is totally controlled because they answer to you and you answer to no one. Because of this, you're thinking:

> "Wow! Who do I want to hire? I want to hire someone who comes from a big company and has a lot of contacts and can operate on their own and be independent and do things without me."

Wrong move! If you go hire someone from an established company like IBM, they're going to fail miserably working in your environment because that's not the environment they're used to and therefore will not find it comfortable. You have to understand that environment is particular and unique to itself, unless you seek a new hire that has experience, and comfort, with this environment. They must be comfortable working in a "loose" environment.

If you're a start-up company, you most likely lack policies and procedures, and you certainly don't have secretaries to do things for you. You don't have administrative assistants, and you don't have the depth of resources of a Fortune100 company. You can't pull a salesperson out of a Fortune100 company, stick them in a start-up company, and expect them to do well. Chances are, they're going to fall flat on their face if that's not their environment. You have to define the Behaviors, Attitudes, Skills Sets and Environment of your company and match it with the salesperson you want to work for you. And put all that down in writing. Have it crystal, crystal clear, no matter how long you have to wait before you are *able* to write it down. I'm not talking about a 1,000-page manual, just the BASE and Comp.

BASE THE COMP ON THE BASE

BASE, in part, should also help you determine your compensation plan. You need a compensation plan that is designed to motivate salespeople to do the things that you want or need them to do. There are hundreds of ways to write comp plans, but we're not really going to get into that in this book. Comp plans constitute enough subject matter for another book.

You need to make sure your comp plan is a combination of salary, commission and bonus. Realize that whatever incentive you lay out for your salesperson, that's what they're going to reach for and achieve.

If it doesn't match, you're either going to fall short and screw them or you're going to get ripped off because you'll have someone make their yearly incentive in a month and put they're feet up on a chair and do nothing but whistle the theme from *The Andy Griffith Show* until their next incentive is placed in front of them.

If you're paying salespeople to get meetings, then they're going to get meetings. If the incentive is based on a quarterly sales, then expect a peak of sales at the end of the quarter. If you're paying them monthly, then expect a peak at the end of the month. You have to make sure that your comp plan is aggressive and focused on rewarding them for doing the right things that you have laid out in your BASE. Comp plans are crucial in this process. BASE and comp plan. Comp plan and BASE. Peanut Butter and Jelly. Jelly and Peanut Butter. Mmm.

While we're talking about comp plans, I think we should go back to the environment component of the BASE. You want to make sure you understand how you're going to manage these salespeople. Are you going to manage them weekly, monthly, or quarterly? Are you going to micromanage them? Or are you going to "seldom-manage" them? You have to understand how you're going to manage your salespeople because this sales perspective has probably been determined by your past more than your present. If you worked at GE three years ago and now you're working for a local car dealership, you might be managing and creating a comp as though you are still at GE. Focus (or re-focus) on the BASE perspective you are creating and looking for now.

The salesperson you're looking for should come from the same or similar environment you want now. Or, they should at least *want* the similar environment that you're looking for *now* (as in, *now* that you have a BASE).

I'm not saying that a person can't come from a different environment and not succeed, but they need to (a) know that it is going to be different and (b) they are going to have to want that change of environment... bad! Real bad.

If you have a micromanaged environment or you are a micromanager, and you have a salesperson that can't be micromanaged, it's not going to work. You have to understand this before you get in the game so you don't go looking for that world of hurt that's coming your way. Similarly, the candidate's idea of a comp plan may be determined by the place where *they* came from, or the place where they *want* to *be*. You can determine that in the ten-minute phone screen which is the first step in the "interview" phase of this process. It's going to be that much easier to identify someone quickly because you will be ready for it.

The beginning of the recruiting process is spent identifying the BASE of the perfect candidate. Understand it's not about what you have now if what you have now is not working. Remember to be objective and really grade your current situation beforehand or it's just more of the same, and twice the pain. This is all about understanding what the perfect candidate *might be*, based on your BASE model. Then, it's time to look at your comp plan as well and see if that needs to be changed. Once you've determined the BASE description of your company and the BASE description of your perfect salesperson, you should combine the two into a list of no less than a hundred items that will help you identify the model for your perfect salesperson. You then have to be willing to say "no" to people who don't fit the BASE model you have created and that you desire. Sales is a game. If you get what you desire, you win. Play to win.

CHAPTER 4
FILL THE POOL

FILL THE POOL

Once you've actually created your BASE model, the next thing you need to do is build a pool of candidates. This pool needs to be large enough so that you are not afraid to kick someone out, and you're not so desperate that you're willing to hire "the next person who comes along." Hiring salespeople has to be done when you don't need to do it. It goes without saying that it's easier to get into one college when another college has accepted you; to get a lover when you have a lover; to get an apartment when you have an apartment; and to get a job when you have a job. The same thing applies here, but later on we are going to have to discuss what you will do if you *need* a salesperson, and you are *desperate*.

The key to getting many things in life is to have the ability to say, "I don't care," or to have the security to say, "no." Otherwise, you seem desperate, needy, erratic, and less focused because the fear and panic takes over and becomes easily apparent to other people. I swear prospects can smell it, and so can salespeople. If you're needy as a hiring company, a good salesperson can sniff it out... especially dogs! Did you ever go into a grocery store when you were hungry? What happens? You buy way too much food, the wrong food, and you probably grab a couple of Ring-Dings in the last aisle and then a Snickers bar in the checkout line while you pay for your useless "groceries." That's when you get a free "snicker" from the pimply teenage bagger or check out guy. Even he can smell it.

The same thing happens when you go and hire a salesperson and you don't have enough to choose from, or you don't have the right mindset, or you're in too much of a rush (desperate). When you're building a pool, it is crucial to build a large pool to choose from, or you're going to dive into shallow water and crack your skull. You certainly don't want to be in the position where you're saying, "Well, it's the best that I could find." That's the old way of thinking and it's pathetic. If you're resorting to that tired excuse, then you definitely are not finding the best and you are not going to any time soon. You simply didn't look hard enough and you didn't have enough to choose from. Basically, what's going to happen is that you'll end up with the same quality person you have now, or worse: you'll end up hiring someone you would fire.

I want you to remember this slogan for the rest of your life:

Never hire those you fire!

... and recite this Limerick each morning and night:

There once was a salesman for hire,
gone searchin' because he was fired.
He answered an ad.
from a desperate lad,
who probably should've retired.

Don't let this be you. In Chapter 9, "Make the Offer" I discuss the kind of applicants you get based on your attitudes regarding salary and comp. This applies at this point as well. There is no special cologne or perfume that can cover the scent of desperation. Actually, there *are* two kinds. I call them *confidence* and *commitment.* You need to be confident that your company is worth working for and that you will offer the appropriate incentives. Through your commitment to this process, you will not appear desperate, but confident. Now you're much more likely to find the great salesperson you are looking for.

THE 100:1 RATIO

Some may say I'm crazy, but I absolutely believe in a 100:1 ratio. There's no doubt you should have 100 people to look at in order to find one good person. Before you slip into a negative state of mind and freak out at the thought of interviewing 100 people, relax and continue. I know that's a lot of people to look at, but right now I'd be more concerned with your methods for building the pool. I've already provided you with a way to weed out 60% of these candidates and it starts with your BASE. The means by which you do the "weeding" is soon on its way. Focus gwasshoppah.

Once you've identified the perfect sales candidate by creating your BASE, you have a couple of different ways to build your pool. At SalesKingdom, we use what we call a "Gatherer," which is a researcher and often a recruiter-in-training. This person's sole responsibility is to fill the pool for SalesKingdom's clients. I surely don't expect to see a full-time gatherer at most companies, but each company at least should have a method for gathering. Think of human evolution from hunter-gatherer to agrarian to communities, city-states, and civilizations. In our company, we tried to think of our most primal, basic ingredients and the gatherer is the start of a larger process. I am not suggesting this job is primal or easy. In fact, it is very demanding and requires an inordinate amount of creativity, resourcefulness, persistence and dedication. Most of all, you need to find someone who truly loves this kind of work. Not all people want to be in sales, but they may want to somehow feel as though they have a greater stake in the company's interests.

This person may be in your company right now. There might be someone you have overlooked, someone who loves to perform the basic requirements of this task, someone who is willing to branch out, maybe receive a small stipend for extra work. The problem is, you won't know how to find a gatherer any easier than you can find a great salesperson unless you know what you're looking for. If this person has to be you, then you must develop a system to gather the information that will start the recruitment process.

Some of these "methods" are listed below, but it is your goal to be creative and think of methods that are not listed here. You also need to consider timing. How long should each step take in this process? I cannot recommend a timeframe because each company is different. It depends upon your resources, your company's current needs and therefore your definition of success. Your definition of success for this process may change each time it is committed.

No matter what you do, try to think of your prospective hires as food. You are going to have to pick a large amount of rotten, inedible apples before you find the one that's going to feed your company, plant a seed and grow. One hundred candidates is going to bring you a lot of rotten apples, but it is the start of a specific process that you are now confident in, and dedicated to playing out to its fullest degree.

BUILDING YOUR POOL:
THE TRADITIONAL METHODS

The first way to build your pool is a fairly traditional method. You run ads on all the job boards (you'll find there are thousands of job boards across the country). These days you'll find the following:

a) Your local paper has a job board built right into it
b) Your local cable company has a job board built right into it.
c) There are a lot of niche job boards out there specific to your industry or your environment.
d) There are a lot of free job boards out there.
e) If you have a problem finding a job board, you will need to *fire your self.*

As a point of interest, you also can find services-for-hire that coordinate and combine all those job boards into one. One of them is called <u>usahire.com</u>. It's a great company and I highly recommend using them if this is the route you decide to take.

They certainly can help you find all the right job boards out there, and writing an Internet ad for job boards is a fantastic plus. That will create a lot of candidates for your pool, but it definitely is not enough, not by a long shot. One of the reasons for this is that it is not a highly creative way to *find* a job, so it is not something that's going to help you find all the best candidates available. You want to place ads in places where you feel creative job seekers will look for jobs, whatever that might mean to you.

The other places to drop ads are your typical newspaper help wanted ads, but don't overlook areas like trade journals. Think of the magazines that people in your industry are reading. For example, I was working for a company that was primarily concerned with the heating, ventilation and air conditioning industry (HVAC). So we found loads of trade journals that a salesperson in that industry might read. They'd be reading journals that talk about new equipment, new products, and new/emerging technologies. We found those journals and we placed ads in those journals.

Get to the salespeople where they are, or where they live. If they're not there already, then they probably aren't doing much to get ahead or to try to stay ahead of the curve in their industry.

Think of what behaviors you want in your salesperson. I'd certainly want mine to be reading magazines or journals from their trade. That's not even creative, it's standard. If you don't know what you want, find another salesperson in your industry and ask them. And, while you're at it, you can see if they're looking for a new job.

WRITING THE AD

Next, you need to decide how to write the ads. If you were to open the paper right now and read ads, you would find that most of the ads describe the *position* they seek to fill. You've seen it so many times that you probably wouldn't even recognize it as your own:

> "We're looking for a salesperson who can sell *blah, blah, blah*, and this position can earn 100K a year, *blah, blah, blah...*"

You and I can get everybody under the sun to respond to that ad (note: dogs), but what you really want is to write the ad to describe the *person* you're looking for. It's the person, not the position. So, go back to your BASE and use that again to create your *person*, not your position. It might sound like this:

> "It ain't braggin' if you back it up!" If this is your motto and you have sold services like office products, office supplies, uniform rentals, cellular/message, telecom solutions, or other office services and are stuck with no upward mobility, then we want to talk to you! The most successful candidate has experience selling to office managers and administrators with 2-3 competitors. You build relationships quickly and want a company that is quality conscious with high integrity. You know how to lead from the front and by example. You have 5+ years of sales experience and are looking for an opportunity to grow in your career. You are a natural motivator and people are attracted to your charisma, style, and leadership. You enjoy the challenge of sales and can transfer your successes to the team! You earn respect instead of expecting it. You understand the importance of sales fundamentals, and are not afraid to get your foot in the door and go head- to- head with the competition. You understand the importance of finding new business and then servicing the accounts you build. You will have opportunities to sell services to financial institutions, law firms, and companies that have a high

level of document confidentiality. This service is recession-proof and growing every day! You must have earned 45k in the past and need to make 60k+. If this ad describes you, e-mail your resume to sarah@saleskingdom.cc.

Try to remember here that you're not just identifying the person you want, but also weeding out the people you do *not* want. The weeds should clearly recognize through this ad that you are looking for someone else, not them. Be warned that in the past, I've written ads that I think were a little intimidating and maybe *too* specific. Don't get too crazy and think that you only want people born on the third Thursday of odd-numbered months during even-numbered years where there was a comet circling 'round the third moon of Jupiter.

I think the only way you can gauge this is to show the ad to salespeople before you send it out. Make sure these salespeople aren't dogs, now that you know how to spot one. Otherwise, you'll just have to gauge it from the amount of hits you get and the reaction you find in the interviews. Yes, you should not be afraid to ask candidates what they thought of your ad. At that point, it's hit or miss and you might need to change it and post it again. There's nothing wrong with failure even at this point. Remember that this is a process and a learning curve. Put yourself out there and try something new. The worst you're probably going to get is what you already have.

Building Your Pool: Head Hunting

Ads are one clear way of building your pool. The other mainstream method for building a pool is to go out and *be* a Head Hunter.

Head hunting is something most companies are very uncomfortable with, but it clearly is one of the best ways to build your pool and the best way to take full, personal responsibility for this piece of the process.

The best way to head hunt is to identify companies that have salespeople that meet your BASE requirement, or generally fit your outlined features. A great place to start is with your competitors. You may find it shady, but it's not illegal and maybe they've already lured a couple of yours away from you without you knowing it. Maybe they've even saved you from having to take your dogs out back...! This is not personal. Remember:

Sales is a Game, Play to Win!

Business is business, and once you have entered this game, you have to treat your employees in a way that stops you from being the one to let your competition return the favor. After this, they'll clearly have the "Screw 'em, he/she did it to me" mindset. Also, keep in mind before you move into this territory that your competitors don't necessarily have the best salespeople. Usually, I find it better to go outside your own industry when you go head hunting.

The best thing to do when head hunting is to first identify the top five companies that would have salespeople that fit your BASE model. You can find them in the least likely of places (this may be your one chance to really get creative). Once you've identified those companies, identify who the salespeople are in those companies. Then identify which salespeople would be interested in making a switch, and get them into your pool. At this point, you better be serious about this. This is not the time to go fishing, thinking you're just going to throw the fish back. You want this fish because you're hungry and know this fish is going to keep you alive. Remember:

Hungry is not desperate!

HEAD HUNTING: MODUS OPERANDI

Know your method of operating or functioning. Consider the following text, which was lifted from SalesKingdom's most recent company website:

It Takes One to Know One

As a recruiting and training company bent on doing things differently, we at SalesKingdom understand that doing business is a creative endeavor, even <u>must</u> be if a business is going to lead and innovate. Unfortunately, most job titles and descriptions do not accurately reflect, and/or actually miscommunicate the actual job content.

From our CEO to Recruiters, and Researchers to our Creative Director, we understand that a business is made up of many different animals, and we lead by leading. Our Jungle/Safari motif reflects that.

The animal that you hire should work for you, not against you. Even the Tamer knows that a Tiger can be "tamed," but one must never forget where that Tiger came from... the Jungle.

By getting to know and describe ourselves we can more accurately get to know your company, its culture, the people who work for you, and the people who should work for you. We know where we sleep, what we eat, and who feeds us... and we won't sleep until we get to know you, too.

So relax and put down that machete. Let us do the work for you, clear the brush that's been weighing you down and blocking your path. SalesKingdom works with you and for you... because we are you... another company hunting for our next meal in the great business herd.

Hungry salespeople know what they want, and what it takes for them to do better and better their position in life. They are not desperate and do not do desperate things because they are confident. You need to be the same. Show prospects you are hungry to do business and to grow your business by only dealing with people who mean business. Either the prospect will connect with that or not.

The only problem with head hunting is that you can immediately kill your chance for adding this person to your pool, simply based on your performance. This is a chance for a salesperson to "audition" *you*, when you are supposed to "audition" *them* much further down the line in this process. Much of this process is based on control and it is hard for you to get control here without being a decent to great salesperson yourself. You must be confident and prepared and show this person you mean business. Be a tiger. Be hungry, but not desperate. If you play the game this way and there is no connection, the prospect is a fish and would flop and flounder in your company anyway. I used to wrestle, and nobody wanted to wrestle what we called a "fish."

In wrestling, a fish flops around the mat and doesn't let you pin him down, hoping that the person in control will either get tired or the time will run out. They're not aggressive and proactive. They're not hungry, just trying to survive. They're passive and reactive. Don't let yourself be a fish, and you will not hire a fish. Are you sick of animal analogies? Too bad, they're still coming. Know what kind of animal you are or what animal you want to be and then *become* that animal. Learn what kind of animal you want to hire and describe it in detail so that the animal that answers your call is indeed the animal that you want and need. Don't send out a goose mating call if you're looking to hunt quail. Quack! Quack!

HEAD HUNTING: NOT FOR THE FAINT-OF-HEART

Let's talk about how you identify salespeople in a company. This part of the process takes a little bit of role-playing, a little bit of strategic thinking, and a little bit of creativity on the phone, but it is well worth the effort.

The best way to identify salespeople is to get on a phone and pretend you're a customer. When you pretend you're a customer, you get sold by salespeople. I suggest you pretend you're a customer and work the system until you learn the names and telephone numbers of every salesperson in the company.

Take this next bit with a grain of salt, because a friend who once researched me arched his eyebrows throughout this whole thing. For those of you who never watched my friend (or virtually anyone who arches their eyebrows), this generally means the person is saying, "Bullshit!" I was working with a company that was trying to hire a salesperson that was currently employed selling in-home carpets. The company had identified a couple of their competitors. They knew they were primarily looking for people who had sold home-improvement items of some kind.

We called up a painting contractor and were delighted to find the contractor had fifteen salespeople. So I let one of my hunters loose on them. He called the contractor, reached the receptionist and said:

"Hi! I'm looking to get an estimate on a house painting. Can you get a salesman after it?" The receptionist said, "Sure, we'll send out Billy Jones." The hunter on the other end replied, "Great, but my husband is a die-hard salesperson, and he's gonna chew up any salesperson you send out. Can you send out the best salesperson you have in your company? I want the very best, the number one salesperson in your company calling us, because my husband will chew up anyone less."

At this point, you would be right to assume that it was not probable for the receptionist to mention the best salesperson right off the bat. The receptionist now changed it to Dean Smith and said, "Dean is the best person we have. We'll send out Dean." The hunter said, "Great. Thank you." But they're not done. Why would they be done? Think of the best catch you could get: "Can I get Dean's cell phone number, just in case, you know, he changes something, or we have to change something at the last minute?" The receptionist says, "Sure, you can." She gave out the cell phone number. Bells ring, a chorus of angels beams their heavenly notes upon us, and the sky opens up. Cell phone number! The crowd goes wild!

Now the Head Hunter has the best salesperson's name and his or her cell phone number. About two hours later, the Head Hunter may call back, and say,

> "Yeah, I have an appointment with one of your salespeople in about three weeks, but yeah, I just can't remember your salesperson's name. Do you have someone there named Patrick? Oh, you don't? Is it, maybe, Peter? No? No Peter here? Then why don't you just go down the names on the list of salespeople in your company and perhaps something will jog my memory. Maybe I'll recognize it then."

Just as quickly as it took you to dial the number, you have a receptionist, the perennial gatekeeper, protector of the arc of the covenant, moving down the list containing every salesperson that the company has on their payroll. Now you can simply say, "Nope, sorry. None of them sound familiar. Must be the wrong company." Click!

The next day or so, the Head Hunter should call back and say, "I'm looking for Salesperson A." You can ask for their last name and say, "Hey! Do you have Salesperson A's cell phone number so I can catch them on the road? Because I think I have an appointment with that person and I might have to reschedule that appointment." Within a few days, you have the first name, last name, and cell phone number for every salesperson in that company. And you have the name of the best salesperson in that company. Will that always work? Hell, no! Does it work enough? If you practice while staying ethical, yes!

HEAD HUNTING: BUILDING INTEREST

You now have targeted a very specific pool of people that you think are going to fit your *environment*. Add these names to the list you compiled from responses to ads and you have successfully identified your pool through head hunting. Once you've identified them, you call them up on their cell phone or at home, or whatever. Don't ask *them* if they're interested in moving to another company. That's a frontal attack and any decent salesperson will see that coming. Also, don't put down their current company, because even unhappy people often have the strange habit of defending what they have now if they are talking to a stranger. It's the old, "This company is a piece of crap, but at least it's still *my* piece of crap." Simply ask the "candidate" if they *know* anyone who is interested in finding a new job. If they do, you'll get that person's name. They may even throw out (or throw up, if they're that easy) an offer to come to you, without ever feeling as though *you're* chasing *them*. They'll feel like *they* are chasing *you*.

If a salesperson thinks you're chasing them, they'll hold out for higher money, higher incentives and everything else. It's unfair negotiation leverage for them and it seriously hurts you. This goes back to my point about having an apartment when you need an apartment... etc. If you go out on a date and you're giving 100% of yourself and acting as though you haven't been on a date in the last five years, you're going to have a hard time getting a second date. People want people who don't *want* them. People want people who don't *need* them. They simply think you do not *accept* them. In our dying need for acceptance, we chase people who run away from us just like *dogs* chase cars and bikes.

You can get what you want in this situation just by saying, "I heard your name from so and so. They said you're a great salesperson and I figured great salespeople know other great salespeople. Do you know anyone who's looking for a job? They'd be selling..." so on, and so forth. This way, if they don't know anyone to refer to you they may willingly offer themselves up for your grab bag. They will feel like they volunteered and you can add them to your candidate pool. In this one transaction, you have effectively stroked their ego (score one) and made them feel unwanted (score two). You also have effectively pulled them toward your favor, and toward a larger candidate pool.

BUILDING THE POOL: REFERRALS

The third way to build a candidate pool is to get the word out to all your referral sources. Think of all your customers as one of the greatest potential sources for candidates. You also want to look toward your prospective clients for referrals. Get the word out to as many people you know that you are looking for a great salesperson. You are *hunting heads*. This is the most cost-effective way to head hunt as well and it keeps you in touch with a lot of important people in your professional and personal life. Use this third strategy to fill your candidate pool to the goal ratio of 100:1 because you have to have at least 100 candidates to find one good salesperson.

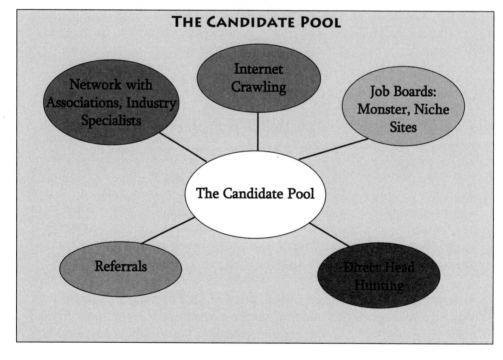

Again, I'd like to bring up the idea that nothing comes for free. I honestly believe you get what you give, even if it has everything to do with business and nothing to do with altruism. The Grinch doesn't get referrals. And just because you're a good guy or gal, don't think you'll get referrals either. It takes more than just a visit with a business card, or a holiday card sent via snail mail, or a monthly e-mail letter.

Refer people to other people in any way you can. Refer people outside your business, occupation or profession. Refer people out of your area of expertise, or hobby or comfort zone. Nothing says you're thinking of someone or that you appreciate someone's services better than an honest referral. By doing so, you place someone else in a brief, trusted advisor position.

Nothing compliments someone's ego more than this simple act. It tells them, "Hey! This guy really wants to know what I think," or "This guy thinks I am the answer to his problems." In this situation, the neighborhood garbage collector becomes the doctor.

Remember that getting referrals takes as much creativity as any other part of this process. I knew a guy who dressed up in some ridiculous costume, usually thematic, every month. He even got his family and dog into it. He had a photo taken, wrote down a brief message and sent it out to everyone he knew, whether they were customers or not. The cards didn't take long to grow a cult-like following and, after a while, he noticed them on people's refrigerators and realized people actually looked forward to seeing him make an ass out of himself each month just to keep in touch. This was never clearer than when he suddenly stopped doing it after more than a year. People were let down and actually complained! Sales takes a lot of networking, and hiring salespeople doesn't take any less if you're doing it right.

Yes, hiring great salespeople is a lot of work, but that's what it's going to take to *make* it work. Remember: proactive, not reactive. This process is a lot less work compared to the work you'll do to replace salespeople every six to nine months because you keep committing the same errors year after year. Besides, nobody said it was easy.

If you want an easy job and think the grass is greener somewhere else, try refilling the Moose Lodge penny fundraising gum dispensing machines at supermarkets. The last time I checked, that was easy. It was uncomfortable seeing my Uncle Rocky doing that job, but my Uncle Rocky never was a good salesperson and he never tried to hire good salespeople either.

The funny thing is, I don't have an Uncle Rocky. But if I did, I certainly wouldn't want that to be *his* job. And I definitely don't want anyone who's read my book to end up that way either! At the expense of using my imaginary Uncle Rocky as a tough-love analogy, I feel we can now move on together, hand in hand, so happy forever. Da, da, da-da-daahhh!

CHAPTER 5
THE PHONE SCREEN

CHAPTER 5

THE PHONE SCREEN

I told you I had a method to save you some actual work, so before you have a panic attack and shut this book forever, let's agree that it's impossible to get 100 candidates in your pool and to interview all 100 candidates. If you still want to hang onto the possibility, then let's agree that it's wasteful or downright stupid. I said it wouldn't be easy, not that it was going to be *insane*. Fearing change is insane.

The key to saving you time and wasted effort is to develop a way to have short, interactive time with these 100 candidates. That's why we use a quick phone screen right off the bat. It's efficient and doesn't require face-to-face time. The phone screen should be ten minutes or less. The point of that phone screen is to talk to the candidate and see if they meet some basic, elementary requirements for you. You want to have ten to fifteen questions prepared which are constructed merely to determine whether or not the candidate has some of the key crucial elements outlined in your BASE model. This is a quiz to weed out the class clowns in order to identify the valedictorian. You're eliminating the fools who think they have it covered and stay up all night boozing and snoozing before the exam.

DEVELOPING THE PHONE SCREEN

These questions should constitute the top ten issues from your BASE model. Look at the 100 requirements you created and pick the ten most crucial to your business, the ten ones that scream, "No matter what, you can't live without me!" We're talking Romeo and Juliet here. You'd rather die than live without them. I don't want you to start a family war, or end up committing suicide in each other's arms. Just make a choice based on true *need*; not lust, love or greed.

Let's say, for example, part of your "environment" concerns in your BASE model suggest the salesperson needs to have experience working with XYZ customers and the next one suggests they need to have a high degree of comfort talking about money. The third concern suggests they need to be comfortable running ten appointments a week and the fourth suggests they need to be comfortable closing the deal themselves. Design ten questions that can identify which salespeople meet your ten most basic requirements for the available position. Using only "yes" or "no" for answers, you will know by their simple 50/50 answers whether or not the candidate has these issues covered.

PHONE SCREEN #1: EXAMPLE

Although it may be a bit long, and may completely differ from the questions you may ask, I'll give you an example of a phone screen used by one of our client companies:

Did you leave each company you worked for on good terms?

What did you sell at each company?

Who did you call on at each company?

What types of services, products, and solutions have you sold in the past?

How long have you been in your present position?

What was your title when you first started with the company?

Who do you report to currently?

What is your title now?

What is your territory?

What types of companies do you sell to at the present time?

Who do you presently call on while on a sales meeting?

What is the average cost of the service or solution you presently sell?

How many cold calls and meetings do you complete in a day?

What is your quota and did you achieve last year's quota?

Are you on target to meet your quota this year?

Are you actively interviewing and do you have any offers on the table at the present time?

What type of sales position are you looking for at the present time?

Remember that each of these questions can be simplified to cut down on the time needed to perform this phase of the process. The whole purpose of this phone interview is not to make friends with the candidate. It's not to become their buddy, or dig into their history too much, or to look at their résumé, or to talk about their experiences. The purpose of this interview is simply to find out if they pass the quick test covering the top ten issues

expertise. Think of a junior high hall monitor giving an Advanced Placement Physics Exam!

For the phone screen, you can get someone who is not even close to being in a hiring position, someone who is not going to be working with a salesperson. Get someone from operations. Get someone from finance. All you want is someone to ask 10-15 questions that are predetermined and get your "yes" or "no" answers. Whether they pass or fail determines whether or not they can move on to the next step. However, you need to be real up front with the candidate, because you don't want them to get nervous and think that they don't even want to go any further. They may end up asking themselves whether or not they really want to take this job, or whether it's worth it to take this job. It may be that this helps you eliminate someone, but there's a difference between challenging someone and simply pissing them off. The real test can come later, when you know you're down to a few choice candidates.

Let the interviewer talk about the test in a more casual manner, using casual tone and perhaps colloquialisms or more laid-back language to put the candidate at ease. And once again, the questioner must assure the candidate that they know nothing about the position. At the end of the questioning, however, they can let the candidate know if they can move on to the next step. At that time, they can reveal more about the *process*, not the *position*.

The interviewer should start out by making sure they have the right personal information, name, phone number, address, e-mail address, etc. Then they can dive into the BASE questions designed by your company. If the candidate passes the BASE test, the interviewer can let the candidate know that the next step will be to have them take either an internet-based or person-to-person sales skills assessment test.

PHONE SCREENING AGENTS

Let me really fly off course here for a minute. If you have a customer service department, or a few agents working in your company that work the phones taking complaints, you may want to consider something here. Customer service can be exactly that: customer service. Lately, however, it seems that customer service has simply become a gateway logjam that keeps good customers away from bad managers; just as honest-to-goodness service agents become effective gateway logjams for bad salespeople who are trying to sell themselves to the company.

Sometimes it's nice for people to step outside the box, switch roles for a minute, and feel as though they're using their skills for something useful. Customer service agents might be perfect for the phone interview. It utilizes their current skills sets, yet allows them to become part of the company hiring process. As gatekeepers, they are great at limiting the potential hire to the objective questioning assigned to them without having to be rude or feel as though they will have to deal with rudeness. At the end of the day, they may feel a different connection with their supervisors and start to build a relationship with someone they may be working with in a short while. In other words, they will feel a different connection with a new hire brought on board by *them.*

Whether it is the customer service people or another department, it is important to keep the phone screen part of the process separate from the final decision maker. The key is to maintain objectivity and compartmentalization. Even my imaginary Uncle Rocky knows this, so remember:

If you separate the people who administer the first steps of the process from those who complete the last steps, you will have much better results.

In recent training sessions and keynote appearances, some trainees and audience members have alerted me to the dangers of putting people through the paces of this process. One point in particular: is it insulting to put great salespeople through simple interviews with anyone less than a hiring manager or VP? I think my most simple answer is, "Who cares?" Let's put this in perspective for a moment and see what we have at stake:

1. You are not hiring your CEO.
2. You are not hiring the CFO, or the COO.
3. You are not hiring a President or a VP.
4. You are not hiring your sales manager.
5. You are hiring a salesperson!

Please note that this process can be and *is* used to hire sales managers every day at SalesKingdom. The requirements for the sales manager position are different for each company that seeks our services, but it works just the same. Typically, the BASE is going to be different. The questions are going to be different. The personality test (or whichever test they choose) is going to be different. The process, however, is going to be structured the same.

First of all, any salesperson or sales manager worth their weight will understand that this process was implemented for a reason. This simply is how your company chooses to handle this all-important situation. If the prospect truly knows what it's like to manage a good salesperson or to be a good salesperson, they will understand. They also should understand that arrogance or a strong sense of entitlement does not make a great salesperson. If you are looking to hire an arrogant person, than you can look for the people that take offense to this process. Make sure the people that implement the test are sure to note it and score it. You can rate these candidates as such:

1. Arrogant Ass (I mean, Ace)
2. King Arrogant Ass
3. Queen Arrogant Ass
4. Arrogant "Jack" Ass
5. Faceless Ass
6. Ass-Cetera

Second of all, titles are given for a reason. If I have a customer service agent who takes part in this process and I dub him "VP of Sales" just prior to the phone interview he is about to conduct, then he is indeed the "VP of Sales." He is clearly doing a task I might require from the VP of Sales and if you think this is dishonest, then I am sorry you feel that way. Everyone in a company is important and no one is above anyone. Certain people simply perform tasks deemed more important or difficult or with greater chance for consequences if mistakes are made. These qualities are judged through company charter and policy and our "title" is a necessary evil of any organization.

If we truly believe that hiring a great salesperson is an all-important task, then this person is all-important and has every right to feel that way and to be treated that way - especially from some Joe Schmoe that doesn't even work for the company...yet. If you feel like this is a white lie or a smudge of the truth, just remember: this "smudge" might help you find a more level-headed, honest, ethical salesperson that will be more level-headed, ethical and honest with your prospects, clients and, eventually, referral sources.

It's my belief that anyone who takes offense to this process probably has unresolved issues that they alone can resolve. They can pay, out of pocket or through insurance, to take care of this problem. You're being paid to find great salespeople and shouldn't have to put up with it. Not now (and because you stood firm at the right point) and certainly not later.

Let's put it another way. In sales, getting an appointment with the CEO is a difficult and rewarding task. So it should be with a salesperson's interview process. Let them be insulted when they're shown the door and you save yourself some much-deserved time, money, and headaches. They'll move on and you'll move on to the next step that brings you closer to finding a great salesperson: the third-party objective test.

CHAPTER 6
BE OBJECTIVE

BE OBJECTIVE

Now you've created your BASE model. You know exactly what your salesperson should look like and you know what avenues you are going to use to find them. You've built a pool of a hundred people and you've screened them over the phone, using your ten to fifteen crucial questions. You should have it whittled down to about *forty candidates*. With these next forty candidates, you can move on to the next step: use a third-party objective tool to test them once again.

There are tons of tests out there on the market today. Many of them are good for certain situations, but you need to do some research and find the one that makes the most sense for you. This again may take some elbow grease, but once you have it, you don't have to look for it the next time. Remember: Uncle Rocky. Gumballs. Keep your resolve here and continue with the process to find your perfect salesperson.

PSYCHOLOGICAL PROFILES

At this stage of the game, you really should be testing the candidate's sales skills and their sales ability. Again, you're going to find a lot of tests that focus on psychological profiles. Target Training International offers some great psychological tests, and Meyers Briggs offers some good ones as well. The problem with psychological tests when talking about salespeople is that a psychological test is not going to tell you how well a person is going to fit in your organization. It's going to tell you if the candidate is emotionally or psychologically stable or schizophrenic.

Well, here's the problem: I can tell you about great salespeople who are psychologically normal and I can tell you about great salespeople who are schizophrenic. If I really had to choose, I'd take the one who consistently brings in the business. Even if they're an emotionally unstable salesperson, they're better than a dog that's stable and brings in nothing. Would you rather have a tiger that bites from the front or a dog that bites you in the ass?

The psychological profile is not going to be anything meaningful when it comes to sales. Did you ever see a crazy man walking down the street? He doesn't care what people think of him! He goes about his business, sometimes blissfully unaware of what's going on around him. I'm not one to take mental illness lightly, but if this crazy man's a musician and he's making beautiful music, let him play on (even if he might also be hearing some awful things in his head).

If your crazy salesperson is making music on the phones, pumping out cold calls, and gaining, let him sell, sell, sell! Don't take the steam out of the choo-choo who could, just because some stupid test says he can't! Coming from an Italian family, I am a great eater. I leave a sorry mess, though, when I'm done. Fact is, I get the job done, though it isn't always pretty. When done with a meal, I am full and happy. And my being full and happy sure as hell compliments the person who cooked the meal. If a person can cook, let 'em cook. There's no greater reward than to sit back and watch the customer eat!

APTITUDE TESTS

Another test you'll see out there is called an aptitude test. Aptitude tests can tell you how much a person knows about sales. However, what they know about sales is entirely different than whether or not they are willing and able to use this knowledge. Here's a great example. Let's pretend Lawrence Taylor from the NY Giants, one of the greatest linebackers in the history of football, held a seminar on being a linebacker. A lot of normal people show up to this seminar. I promise you that at the end of the seminar the participants all could take an aptitude test about linebackers and score extremely well. After all, they have learned, from a master, what it's like to be a great linebacker. They would have learned all the key plays, key moves, and all the things a great linebacker needs to work at. I guarantee, however, that they're not going to go out and play for the NY Giants tomorrow. They're going to get their butt whooped.

Just because you know about or study something, doesn't mean you can do it. There's a big difference. Aptitude in sales is no different. Just because you know *how* to sell doesn't mean you *can* sell. You don't just want an aptitude test, you want a test that can tell you whether or not the candidate can apply that knowledge and use the necessary techniques. You can test for these skills in a live interview, *later.*

BEHAVIORAL TESTS

Behavioral tests are another tool you can use for a candidate search. These are going to tell you whether or not people are organized or disorganized, detail-oriented or not detail-oriented. Once again, as far as they relate to sales skills, behavioral tests are irrelevant. I've seen organized and unorganized salespeople. Hell, I've helped train unorganized salespeople how to *be* more organized. In some cases it just screwed them up.

A system's not a system if it isn't the system a person creates for him or herself!

I've seen neat and sloppy salespeople, *all* excellent salespeople. In most cases, a person's organizational habits had no bearing on their sales skills. In any case where it did have bearing, they were probably just a dog and needed to be led out back and… If not, that dog needed to be taught a new trick. And remember, that dog may be you!

Now that we're here, what we're really looking for is to understand the candidate's sales skills and to make sure they have some of the right attitudes that we're looking for. No matter which test you use, it is crucial that you now bring in another third-party objective opinion. Compare your candidates objectively and rank them objectively, because now you want to find a way to drill down even further. You can't be interviewing thirty people for the full-term interview process that we're going to get to in *Chapter 7: The Interview.* You have to cull that list even further. This test will give you an objective comparison.

There's another thing about this test you must remember. When you get to this group of candidates, you can't test half of them or a third of them. You must test *all* of them. It will not work as intended if you do not follow through with this advice. After you phone screen the candidates, you have to ensure that everyone, whether it's ten, twenty, or thirty people, is tested the same way. You must do this in order to know in your heart that you were objective.

PeopleAnswers

At SalesKingdom, we use a third-party test from a company called PeopleAnswers. We use this test because it is the most effective all-around test out there, combining the psychological, aptitude and behavioral aspects of other tests. It is simple to use, simple to pay for and gives consistent, objective results. Their test will take the prospect an hour to complete at most and

PEOPLE ANSWERS ASSESSMENT
Measures:
◆ Intellect
◆ Drive and Motivation
◆ Work Style
◆ Interpersonal Skill
◆ Leadership/Management Style
◆ Culture Fit

if it takes more than that, you'll know the prospect isn't quick enough on their feet and you don't want/need them.

PeopleAnswers is the leading provider of web-based behavioral assessment solutions, allowing for efficient and methodical selection and development of top performers at all professional, managerial, and customer facing levels of your company. They can give you great insight into your candidates as well as your current employees. Their software will help you compare a candidate with your company's own customized BASE profile, which will help you find your tigers and sniff out your dogs.

TIPS

Check out this website for more information:
www.talentmgtgroup.com.

PeopleAnswers: *Culture Fit Example*

The following is a mock *culture fit* example for my imaginary Uncle Rocky. Here, you will see just one summary page out of more than forty pages that will constitute your total report from PeopleAnswers. They are in-depth informational assessments that are extremely helpful, especially when used in conjunction with the SalesKingdom recruitment process. At the end of the summary, you may decide if Uncle Rocky is fit to sell gumballs or if he should instead make the choice to move on to the next phase of the process and come to work for you!

Management Suggestions for Culture Fit
Imaginary Uncle Rocky

The following paragraphs detail management suggestions for guiding

Uncle Rocky through the issues raised in the Impact at Work narrative for the Culture Fit competency. Uncle Rocky prefers a fairly casual environment and is highly tolerant of job-related pressure and stress. Uncle Rocky will approach his daily work with relative seriousness, but his playfulness and humor will likely provide him an outlet at project "down times"; you should adjust your approach to him appropriately. Since Uncle Rocky works well under excessive stress, he is a natural choice for situations where timelines or project requirements are extreme. Some teammates may be thrown by Uncle Rocky's ability to shift quickly between serious intent and playful behavior, so it may be helpful to assign him to teams where at least some members have previous experience working with him. While Uncle Rocky's stress tolerance is high, you should be careful to monitor him for burnout, as the symptoms are likely to be subtler than in the average employee.

Uncle Rocky thrives in an environment without known structure and is comfortable making reasonable adjustments in his duties or schedule. Uncle Rocky works very well without clear lines of authority and will respond best if able to go directly to whomever he needs to speak without having to work up through numerous levels. In general, he will adapt easily to mergers and acquisitions, but you should provide him a lot of information. Without such information, he may be slightly more resistant than employees with a higher tolerance for work shifts. Other people may not respond well to Uncle Rocky's comfort with breaking the chain of command and approaching others without regard to position or authority. For this reason you may need to help him be attuned enough to organizational politics not to get burned. Be aware that Uncle Rocky may request additional information about organizational or position shifts as he determines his attitude toward the adjustments.

Uncle Rocky is open to new ideas and strategies and is extremely competitive both internally and externally. Uncle Rocky likes to strike a balance between the tradition of the organization and innovative ideas and strategies. When sacrificing one for the other, be sure you are able to communicate a clear rationale. Uncle Rocky competes openly and comfortably for position, salary, perks and any other valuable incentive; use these items as very powerful rewards only when truly earned. While committed to expanding the organization, Uncle Rocky will not easily support ideas that disregard the standard strategies of the organization. Alienation of less competitive employees may be a concern with Uncle

Rocky, so work with him to tone down his competitive nature when inappropriate or overwhelming to others.

Overall, Uncle Rocky works well at a moderate pace. Rather than being at any consistent pace, his style will likely include periods of rapid, high-energy work interspersed with times of lower-level speed. You should monitor and evaluate his overall accomplishments rather than be concerned about his daily pace. Since Uncle Rocky's preferred pace is ever-changing, he is best assigned to projects where there is some independence for group members and the entire group is not required to move forward at the same pace.

Uncle Rocky enjoys socializing with his co-workers but does not want to become overly involved with them. Uncle Rocky likes social activities for specific events such as holiday parties or going away parties and may be a very good volunteer for organizing these occasional get-togethers. Be cautious of overburdening Uncle Rocky with social responsibilities as he may burn out quickly.

USEFUL IN THE RIGHT HANDS

Use this information wisely, no matter which company you choose to provide the information. But beware: impostors abound! It is easy for someone to give their password to a friend, family member or colleague so they may take the test for them. In our next chapter, we will talk about "testing the test," whereby you can try to catch the cheaters, but at this point you need to assume that everyone has been honest.

When all of your candidates have taken this third-party objective test, you will have a great, objective way to rank these candidates. Rank them separately based on the results of this test, as well as their phone screen from the previous step/chapter, and number the results from each test, 1-20. Once you have those separate lists and scores, you can then combine the two (average them) and rank them from top to bottom. Now you have two objective scoring methods combined for one ranking, so you should be sure that you could move on to step five, which is the *Full-Length Phone Interview*.

Now you're going to give them a chance to go to the dance, but you need someone to take their golden ticket and make sure it's the real deal, straight outta the chocolate factory. Doompadee doo!

CHAPTER 7
THE INTERVIEW

CHAPTER 7

THE INTERVIEW

A t this point, you should have a minimum of ten people and a maximum of thirty. This stage of the game requires you to take the remaining candidates and have a longer, more in-depth interview. This interview can be done over the phone or face-to-face, whichever is preferred for your own personal benefit. Either way, it doesn't matter. This is not what suits me. It's what suits you. If you wish, you may flip to the end of this chapter before reading on. There, you'll find an example of a full-length phone interview with some following remarks to close out this chapter. It may or may not help you to read those questions first and return back here afterward.

FIVE THINGS TO TEST FOR

1. TEST THE TEST

There are five things you want to test in this interview. First, you want to "test the test." You're going to want to rule out the possibility that these people could have had someone else take the third-party objective test we discussed in the previous chapter. Remember that salespeople are crafty and they will always try to beat the system, whether it is through ethical or unethical means. I have seen many candidates who have had their best friend take the test. Ultimately, I suppose they thought their "friend" could obtain a higher score than they would achieve. Believe me, it happens. My good ol' Uncle Rocky tried to have Cousin Timmy take the test for him. Look where he ended up.

Ask the candidate some of the questions they answered from the first test and cross-reference the answers they give you, yet rephrase some questions so they clearly are not the same questions from the previous test. You want to look for inconsistencies in their answers. If there are, kick the candidate right out. Ethics is of high importance in any employee and if they cheat now they will cheat later. Take them to the shed and pull the trigger. Or pay later to have them hunted down somewhere in Argentina with a bottle of hair dye in one hand and a Mai Tai umbrella in the other, all paid for on your corporate account.

2A. PAST BEHAVIORS

The second thing you want to test for in the interview is the behaviors that they have done in the past. Salespeople are creatures of habit. If they have maintained a certain level and style of behaviors in the past it is a safe bet they will repeat these behaviors. Like a good poker player, avoid tipping off your hand or telegraphing your moves. Do this at all costs! Never tell the candidate the types of behaviors you are looking for; rather, make them tell you what behaviors they have exhibited in the past.

If you tell them what you are looking for, expect that they will tell you, "Oh, yes. I can do that." They'll "yes" you to death. Did you ever watch the play/movie *Glengarry Glenn Ross*? If you have, try to remember and think of the George Aaronow character: "Shoes. Boots. Yes." If you haven't seen this play/movie yet, climb out of the hole you've been in and get a membership to a good video store. Or better yet, get out and see an actual play! Theater is role-playing, (which is one of the best ways for sales-people to improve their skills) and there's nothing better than for you to see this role-playing, live! This particular play/movie is a great educational tool, as you will learn the following:

a. The wrong way to manage your salespeople
b. How every salesperson *might* feel about you
c. What true dogs, horses and tigers look like in action
d. The most unethical sales behavior possible

One of the best ways to avoid detection is to have the salesperson write out what a typical month would look like in their last job. This way, they can't get a handle on what you will expect from them.

Ask them to focus on detailing the behaviors they would have been doing. Look for the number of calls, meetings, proposals, e-mails, etc. Keep a sharp eye out for a salesperson listing things like internal meetings, proposal writing, report writing, and production meetings. If the candidate does not immediately focus on the sales behaviors, it is a good indicator that they are not going to focus on them when they work for you.

2B. THE 30, 60 & 90-DAY PLAN

After they make a list of the things they did when they worked at their old job, have them make a list of the actions and behaviors they would expect to exhibit if they came to work for you. Have them list, in detail, a 30, 60 and 90-day plan with specific focus on behaviors. This is where things will get difficult. You can't teach a horse to eat meat. It's a grass eater. The same thing applies to a salesperson. If you have a person who is used to running five appointments per week while making about twenty calls a day and you need them to be on fifteen appointments per week while making thirty calls per day, you will not get them there.

Don't kid yourself and think you can "grow" salespeople. Though both are perfectly beautiful carbon-based life forms, people and plants do not share enough DNA, and you don't have 3.78 billion years to wait for a proper mutation. In the spirit of separation of church and state, *do not wait for an act of God!*

The only time you "grow" people is when they are already on the team and it is more costly to replace them than it is to train them. If a poor performer has a modest amount of talent that can be tapped and focused, you might be able to whip 'im (train him) and hold him acutely accountable for certain behaviors (whip 'im) and get some okay results (because he still prefers grass to meat). Remember that this takes a lot more energy than training a talented person with proven, exhibited behaviors that does not need to be held accountable. Let me say this once, for the record:

Training, in general, should only be reserved for people who do/are doing well and can do better because they have the twin golden chalices named talent <u>and</u> dedication. Anything else is a clear waste of time, money and patience.

If you are already in the replacement mode, then fire your filthy dogs and hire the best damn "A" player you can hire.

3A. Testing for Attitudes: Money

After you have tested the test and confirmed the behaviors, it's time to test for the attitudes. The first attitude to test for is the money attitude. If you could, you would want to walk into your sales candidate's house and sit down to dinner with their husband or wife. And just as they're about to take a bite of the lovely pot roast, you'd say, "Nice house. Can I ask you how much you paid for it?" Let me present with you three different sales-people:

> a) In the blink of an eye, *Salesperson A* says, " 250K," and goes on to tell you all about the interest rate, the property taxes, the water bill, trash removal, etc.

> b) After a rub of their chin, *Salesperson B* says, "Ah, it was a pretty penny, but we saved up a bit and managed."

> c) *Salesperson C*, being the calm, collected, tight-lipped person they are, gasps and spits a hunk of food across the room, and moans loudly about how much they paid for the on-sale table cloth they just stained with a half-digested hunk of pot roast.

This simple test will let you know their comfort level when talking about money. Of course, the sales dog might just say nothing, or, "Please pass the bone salad." Aarf! Aarf!

3B. Testing for Attitudes: Decisions

Testing for the decision attitude is very simple. Simply ask the candidate about the last major purchase they made and how they made it. Listen for them to say they shopped around and compared prices and purchased based on the best price. Even lead toward this answer. If they say they did not shop, prompt them with questions that show you are surprised they did not shop.

The key to discovering the candidate's decision-making attitude is that the candidate's buying decision should perfectly exhibit how they will help their prospect make a buying decision. You want the salesperson's decision attitude to match the decision cycle you expect from your prospects. It's a simple rule of human behavior. All human beings impose their beliefs on others either consciously or unconsciously. It's warped, but true. We all, in a sense, are day-sleepers, completely unaware of our most important so-called "waking decisions."

3C. TESTING FOR ATTITUDES: NEED FOR APPROVAL

The third attitude to test for is the need for approval. This also is simple. Describe a situation to the candidate that would represent the ultimate buying situation. For example: "Pretend that you had met with the decision maker of a company about the product you are selling. They need the product, it is a perfect fit for them, they have the budget and the person you are talking to is the decision maker." Next, have the candidate rank these four optional outcomes from the sales call:

1. A "Yes" Answer
2. A "No" Answer
3. A Future Meeting
4. A New Friend

If the candidate ranks these options in any other order than 1,2,3,4, as listed above, they clearly show a need for approval. The higher the candidate ranks "A New Friend," the greater their need for approval in sales because we all know making friends does not make sales. Making friends gets you an "in" with the supermarket bagboy responsible for unlocking the gumball machine that Uncle Rocky has cornered anyway. You get nothing! In all seriousness, this may sound like a simple test that salespeople will ace but in our experience, most salespeople have never seen it and tend to answer it incorrectly. It is a great way to throw up a caution sign and initiate further review of this attitude. Remember: caution signs are good...for you. Cautions signs help you to stay objective.

To a salesperson with no need for approval, a client's "no" is just as good as a "yes" and you know the fear of rejection is very low. If you have a sales cycle with a lot of rejection, you have to make sure your candidate has a very low need for approval or they will quickly self-destruct in the future. Nothing's as sad as watching a person self-destruct, especially when you know *you* may be responsible because you weren't equipped to make a good hire. Hearing "no" on a constant basis will grate on most people's nerves and literally weakens their spine. Eventually, they can lose their taste for the profession in its entirety. That's when you see total "life reconstruction."

I'm going to ask you to run with the mental illness analogy once again. Think of homeless people on the street begging for people's spare change. Think of the guy who wants to sell you a joke for a dollar, or get you to pay for that "bus ticket home." Did you ever hear that one? No one hears "no" more than beggars. They are cold-calling and prospecting all day long. I've even had friends "refer" me to certain homeless people because they actually do something constructive with their money and prove it to their regulars. To handle constant rejection, you either have to be mentally ill or be very strong, confident and able to separate your business life from your personal life. You can't take rejection personally.

3D. TESTING FOR ATTITUDES: EMOTIONAL DISCIPLINE

The final attitude to test for is the emotional discipline attitude. Depending on how much pressure there is in the sales cycle, you will need to have differing degrees of emotional discipline in your sales force. The best way to test this is a lot of fun for the interviewer but really painful for the candidate. I am a little bit of a masochist, so I have a blast with this. Now that I think of it, that rhyme might be the greatest I ever came up with: Masochist. Blast with this. Maybe even, blasphemous?

I digress once again. Anyway, when the meeting seems to be going along well and things are at a very relaxed pace I simply ask, "On a scale of 1-10, how would you rank the progress of this interview?" The candidate drops the proverbial, "Oh, it's a 9.5, and when you decide to hire me it will be a 10 for both of us." That's when I like to drop the, "What would you say if I said it was a 2?" This answer shows this salesperson may be a new crossbreed of dog and donkey. Ask yourself: "Would I say something so cheesy, smarmy and presumptuous?"

Now it is time to sit still. Watch their ears turn red. See them fidget in their chair. Witness the sweat on their upper lip. Observe the frantic tap of their leg. Behold, the dog at the dinner table. They don't really know if you're ever going to throw them a bone. This lets you know that the candidate takes things too personally and they just lost control of their emotions. This can be lots of fun. Okay. Let me gather myself for a minute, here. You may feel like a jerk, but any salesperson worth a second chance will pull out of it. Don't make me tell you the pathetic things I said in interviews over the years! Again, I'm speaking from experience, and now I am the one behind the big oak desk. Admit it. It's a different view, isn't it?

4. TESTING FOR SKILLS SETS

I could write a whole book on how you might test for Skills Sets. That is not a joke or even intended to be slightly humorous. My editor, however, would not let me leave it out in the recruiting context, so I agreed to give the Reader's Digest version. Understand that you have already tested for their skills sets, in some form, in all previous steps of this process. You have identified skills sets you are looking for and you've made your BASE list (this is the process repeating itself for further clarity). Now you need to simply ask the prospect general questions so they can confirm or deny they have this skills set. No, this is not rocket science. If you have used an adequate skills sets assessment tool in the previous steps you will have a good idea of their skills sets already. You are simply looking to get a subjective confirmation or denial for the skills sets you are looking for. The easiest way to do this is to make a list of the top twenty-five skills sets you are concerned with. Design questions to test for each skills set and in your interview process, ask the questions to determine if they have the skills sets or not. Note here that in the next step, you will require them to prove it.

5. TESTING FOR MATCHING ENVIRONMENTS

The environment portion of the interview is one of the hardest for most people to employ. It is hard because it is personal. As an employer you must be brutally honest with yourself about the environment you have to offer. Let's face reality here. Not every company is so flush with cash that they have the most magnificent office loaded with administrative support and a personal secretary for each salesperson. Also, the overloaded manager of today may get frustrated and stressed and ignore or abuse the salespeople on the team. I know it is a cliché, but you are a juggler, expected to keep one eye on everything and something somewhere will suffer for it. It may be the one or two most important things in your business life.

Unfortunately, this may affect your personal life as well.

If you are going to hire and/or manage salespeople, you must be honest with yourself. One of the biggest reasons for salespeople's failure is not of their own making. Usually, the person who hired them is not capable of managing them. The person who hired them may not be an adequate manager and they may destroy an otherwise good salesperson. Take a long hard look. Do you avoid mirrors? Are you a vampire without a reflection? Are you ready to come clean and join the world of the living?

It may be that in the past, certain salespeople were left to their own devices, never observed in the field. They were like ghosts and these "mavericks" might kick butt in certain environments. Adversely, they might be expecting you to micromanage them. Again, if you must, take some classes to whip your own butt into shape. Come clean, realize your own strengths and weaknesses, and learn what you/the company wants beforehand and you will save yourself a lot of trouble. And learn what you can do to be more effective.

Once you have wiped away the tears from your own company therapy session and you have a good understanding of your real environment, you now can make it a little bit tougher and describe this to the candidate. If you are a close manager, tell them that you are a micromanager. If you have a little admin support to offer, tell them you have none.

 One of the "safest" moves you can play in this game is to downplay the environment and look for the salesperson to still keep coming at it. Make the salesperson convince you that they are able to work in your difficult environment and be successful.

What happens once they've taken the job and realize things are a little bit better than they expected? Well, that's just gravy, isn't it? It may be tougher than you think, regardless.

I hate to be tough here, but if you think your work environment is not tough, let me ask your existing salespeople. I am sure I will come up with a mile-long list of reasons they think the environment does not support them. Don't worry! Every environment has its challenges, but we don't want to set the wrong expectations for later.

Let's talk about the most pure example of the perfect, puritan, work environment the United States has to offer the world: *The Magic Kingdom.* Do you honestly think every Disney employee smiles in those labyrinthine tunnels and offices underneath the Magic Kingdom the same way they do above ground in the park? Ask Jeffrey Katzenberg. For his autobiography, he got over (around) his confidentiality waiver. Excuse me… agreement.

Remember that there are only three reasons why your employees don't file legitimate complaints or offer suggestions regarding your performance:

1. You have the authority to fire them.
2. You have the authority to fire them.
3. You have the authority to fire them.

Okay, in all seriousness:

1. You videotaped their bachelor party.
2. You were their college roommate and are the only one to truly understand what they mean by "experimented."
3. You prepare their food each day and have an intimate knowledge of hard-to-trace lethal chemicals.

Okay, in all genuine seriousness, every employee of every company has a gripe to file with their superiors, no matter who they are or how they do business. This is mainly because most people are not at the top and do not have the balls to complain, other than to prairie dog over the cubicle wall to complain to the hedgehog next to them. Whole cartoon series have been written regarding these subjects and people love them because they are *true.*

Every supervisor can represent the stern father from the employee's childhood, or the bastard aunt, the snooty professor, the moron that cut them off in the parking lot, the jerk who wouldn't hold the elevator for them, or the jackass next door who won't shave the tree branches littering your yard with impossibly difficult-to-rake leaves. Phew!

PHONE INTERVIEW: PAST EXAMPLE

The following is a loose example of an interview outline you can use to interview the candidate either face-to-face or over the phone. Remember that you can redesign each question to elicit a simple yes/no or true/false answer. This saves time and eliminates gray areas. However, a good salesperson can take control through actual skills, the same skills as you are checking.

BEHAVIORS

1. Who do you report to at the present time? What is your relationship with that person?
2. How do you track yourself?
3. How do you prepare yourself for your week?
4. What does a typical day look like in your world?
5. How many meetings did you go on last week and what were the outcomes?
6. How many meetings do you have scheduled for this week and next?
7. How many sales did you make last year?
8. How many new customers did you bring in last year?

ATTITUDES

1. What are your goals? Are they in writing?
2. Where do you see yourself in three, five, and ten years from now?
3. Pick a specific sales accomplishment and tell me about it.
4. If I were to ask a fellow co-worker or client about you, what would they say?
5. What do you consider to be your greatest strength? Weakness?
6. Tell me about your last large purchase, not including a car or house.
7. How long did it take you to buy it?
8. How many places did you go to?
9. Where did you end up buying it from and why did you buy it from there (cost, quantity, quality)?
10. What is the hardest thing you have had to do in your lifetime?
11. What are you passionate about?
12. What do you like to do outside the office?
13. What is more important: getting the business -or- not getting the business?
14. Rank the following in order of importance:
    1. Get the business
    2. Don't get the business
    3. An opportunity to go back
    4. Make a friend

PHONE INTERVIEW: PAST EXAMPLE (CONT.)

SKILLS

1. How do you prospect?
2. What is your sales style?
3. How does it feel when someone rejects you?
4. How long does it take you to get over rejection?
5. How do you generate business? (Not leads, but closed deals.)
6. Walk me through your sales process.
7. Why does someone buy from you?
8. Have you had sales training? Describe it.
9. Walk me through your sales process from the time you prospect the client to closing the deal.
10. Discuss the largest deal you have sold.
11. What is the average size deal with your present company?

ENVIRONMENT

1. What type of environment do you excel in (micromanaged, autonomous, structured)?
2. Tell me something you liked about your favorite boss and your least favorite boss.
3. How do you rank amongst your peers?
4. Companies have strengths and weaknesses. What are some things your present company could do to be more successful?
5. Do you like selling and account management or just selling the deal and moving on to the next prospect?

SALARY HISTORY / EXPECTATIONS

1. What is your current compensation package at your present job?

   a. Base
   b. Commission
   c. Bonus
   d. Car Allowance
   e. Cell Allowance
   f. Laptop
   g. 401k
   h. Vacation
   i. Expense Plan
   j. Medical, Dental, Vision Insurance
   k. Other

2. What is the most money you have made? When?
3. What do you want to make?
4. What do you need to make to pay your bills?
5. How do you think this interview is going?
6. When would you be able to start in a new position?

HOMEWORK

1. Prepare a research project using Microsoft Power Point. This project should be a 30, 60, and 90-day work plan for a hypothetical company.

REFERENCES

See text on next page.

SEND 'EM BACK TO SCHOOL

If you notice, we have listed "homework" and "references" at the end of the hour-long phone interview. If you do not believe the candidate qualifies after this step, you should once again thank them for their time and effort and let them know they are no longer being considered for the position. If you wish, you may opt for a respectful, well-written letter that is a bit more personal than your average rejection letter. If you believe the candidate is still qualified and ready for the next step, you may opt to discuss or "clear-up" their references.

If there's anything in their reference materials that bothers you at this point, you know for certain it is a waste of time to continue unless you are 100% sure everything is clean. You may be objective and decide that anything less than perfect disqualifies a candidate. Or you can be subjective, using part logic and part instinct to decide if the candidate deserves more time or more questioning to clear any inconsistencies or to gather additional information. And of course, you should get an objective, third-party opinion regarding your decision, either way.

If a person has been asked for references, they should have them relatively quick, if not immediately. The amount of time you give them may depend on the candidate's circumstances, though I still believe that most great salespeople will have them available at all times. This is one easy way to identify either a Tiger or a Con Artist. However, you must remember that we discussed real down and dirty head hunting in *Chapter 4: Fill the Pool*. If you're head hunting and grab a decent salesperson by surprise, you should expect that they need a little time to get their act together and update/revise their employment records. It certainly depends on how stringent you are with your needs, including the following:

a) The amount of time you give the candidate to obtain records
b) How timely the information should be, such as reference letters from within the past year only
c) If you require information that is dependant upon third-party companies or institutions, such as school transcripts, credit reports, drug tests, etc.

If you already know everything is in order, you may want to assign a "research project" to the candidate. At SalesKingdom, we suggest this for a good portion of the sales positions we fill each year. Again, if the candidate is insulted or put off, good! This is an easy way to bounce them from the process. Any organized, dedicated salesperson already has most of this project assembled in some form, somewhere. If they're real good, they already have it done or can easily put this together in a very short amount of time. Regardless, it's safe to say they might be able to use it somewhere down the line for another interview.

I have a friend in public relations who has been asked to complete research projects as part of the interview process. The companies he applies to almost always ask for writing samples and, quite often, actually give live writing tests (see next chapter: *The Audition*). After five harmless interviews, all of which were great learning experiences, he had a basic portfolio he could show future prospective employers. As he gets better at his game, he continually updates each sample and furthers his ability to get a job in the future.

Public relations is very similar to sales in that it is a profession where head hunting is rampant, all-present, and actually either *accepted,* or at least *expected.* Remember: it's just business. If you are still worrying about "bothering" the candidates, then you have lost the game and should turn back and start over. Or give up. Thank you. Nice try. I'll be happy to give you Uncle Rocky's gumball business number and better yet... a reference. You may be perfect for the job.

If you want the perfect salesperson for your business, get over your fear of rejection and try giving them a test. Like everything in this process, you're going to figure out:

      a.) What you want them to research;
      b.) How you want them to format the research;
      c.) A reasonable timeframe for them to accomplish the research.

You should consider which software you want the candidate to use to submit their homework, such as word processing, spreadsheet or presentation software. Also consider what medium you want them to use for submission, such as Internet, hard copy, snail mail, fax, etc. Consider the benefitts for all your choices. For our research project, we usually ask candidates to prepare their own 30, 60 and 90-day work plan for one of the following:

a) The company for which they are applying

b) One of the hiring company's competitors

c) A company in a different field or profession

d) A hypothetical company

There are many benefits to using any of the above choices, which would be too complex and lengthy to discuss here. In any case, the choice usually depends on the information the hiring company wishes to learn or extract and is based on both the company's personalized BASE profile, as well as the candidate's responses to prior stages of the process. This especially includes, but is not limited to the PeopleAnswers test and the full-length phone interview.

RESEARCH PROJECTS
EXAMPLES:

♦ 30, 60 and 90-Day Action Plan

♦ Research the industry and outline a step-by-step, detailed sales strategy for this particular position.

♦ Brainstorm: How many contacts do they have that they have already established throughout their career that they could approach about this particular product or service?

We almost always ask our candidates to use Microsoft PowerPoint to present their research because we want to keep our available options. Again, this includes but is not limited to the candidate's live presentation to the hiring company. This is a great option in the "Audition" which we will get to in a moment because it gives the candidate an opportunity to present and sell, just as they would in an actual, on-the-job sales presentation.

Don't forget to closely examine your questions before you ask them in the hour-long interview. This will ensure you are precise, laser-focused, and do not allow too much room for subjectivity. You may want to do role-plays before you go "live" with these questions and definitely make sure you time it. See how much room the candidate will have to "squirm" or "dodge" these questions, or identify those that allow the candidate to avoid giving real, straightforward answers.

You also should note that the above sample questions we gave you are very similar to those we presented for the 10-minute phone screen. The short interview is usually a whittled down version of the larger test, where you get into the real specific BASE questions. This is purposeful and helps you "test the test." If you want more simple answers for any question, simply turn them into a "yes" or "no" question. For example:

"How do you like to be managed?"

becomes...

"Do you like to be micromanaged?"

You should only ask a person a yes/no question if you are mainly concerned with a direct hit/match or an opposite reaction/answer. If you *want* a person to like being micromanaged, ask them this question. If you *don't want* a person who likes to be micromanaged, you can ask them this question. Just remember that some questions will give direct answers without having to be yes/no questions. If you ask a candidate what field they work in, you can get a very direct answer without eliciting a yes/no response.

If you are looking for something else, such as something hazy, subjective or in between, design another question to make it more black and white. Or design another question that helps focus on the answer you wish to receive. You'll find that PeopleAnswers does a good job with this, but remember that their test is done on the computer. Your test is conducted by a human, which gives you more flexibility and the chance for you to use your instincts, which may be what you're looking for.

The interview is now over and you need to have a preset expectation or definition of the phrase "passing the interview." This determination can be assisted by the "grade" they receive on their research project. Or, just as with every other step in this process, make sure you designate *one* person to "score" or "grade" the candidate's performance.

Regardless of your method of execution, the candidate needs to match a certain percentage of the BASE model in order to go to the next level. We use the following two criteria:

1. We want to pick the top five to go on to the next level, and/or...
2. There must be a minimum 65% match to qualify.

If this is not the case, then it's back to the drawing board. Yes, that means you need to start the whole process over again. If not, it is up to you to take any and all responsibility for these candidates' failure if and when they are hired. I'm not saying that the #6 candidate or a 64.5% match cannot succeed, but in a more pessimistic view you need to know that they are .5% more likely to fail. By the way, my numbers were not determined through the SWAG Method (Scientific, Wild-Ass Guessing), but several years' worth of data and experience in the recruiting business. You can take this advice or leave it, but come clean and own up to it. No scapegoats, no excuses. If you won't lose sleep at night and you are convinced you did everything you could to stick with the process, then it's time for the real fun to begin... the *Audition*!

CHAPTER 8
THE AUDITION

THE AUDITION

You've worked hard and are about to enjoy the fruits of your labor. Now the real fun begins. Okay, I know it's *all* fun, but the last part of this process is where the rubber meets the road and you get to see for real if the candidate is a Tiger, a Horse, or a dirty old Dog with fleas. Remember the Western's where the outlaw spits on the dogs with chaw and buckshot? If the candidate made it this far, however, you have a general belief that they match your BASE enough to be a successful candidate.

Save the spitting for Clint and company. In reality, your dog candidates should be dead and buried and your horse candidates are quietly grazing on some land owned by a motion picture studio head who doesn't understand the meaning of "An offer you can't refuse." The audition is set up to see if the candidate actually performs the *behaviors* and displays the *attitudes* and *skills sets* within the *environment* that resembles the environment they may be joining. This means *your* environment. And again, this is no time to get lazy.

The tightrope that you will walk during this part of the process will push the candidate hard enough to make them truly display the attributes you want to see without having to overdo it. By now the candidate has put in a lot of time and you don't want to kill them. These candidates are the cream of the crop and you should have a good relationship with them by now. Just make sure it's still a business relationship and you *are not* exemplifying the typical dog-like behavior you may have had before you read this book.

As with every step in this process, it is impossible to describe every way to audition the candidate, so I will once again stick with the Reader's Digest version (my editor hates that analogy). I will show you five ways to audition the candidate to see if they live up to your expectations and if they really do pass "the test." Nerves run high here, so you can push them hard but give them a small break when judging their "performance." If you're a movie buff, you'll know that many actors originally were not chosen for their most famous roles. After the movie becomes a classic, we can hardly imagine another actor filling the role. The director or producer gave them a chance because they knew they had something they could use. This portion of our process can be very black and white and subjective at the same time.

One huge mistake people make in face-to-face sales interviews is being too darn nice. Does a kid respect a father or a pal? It's unfortunate that most people conduct a sales interview in the following manner:

1. Invite the candidate in
2. Sit them down like they were a date
3. Make them coffee (like you're running a bed and breakfast)
4. Chitchat with them (like you're a parent of the bride)
5. Ask them about their family
6. Send the candidate out the door (with a slice of their mom's best meatloaf)
7. Throw confetti over the candidate's head on the way to their car
8. Throw down your jacket to assist the candidate over a puddle lying next to the their car!
9. Pat the car as the candidate takes off into the sunset, laughing all the way to *your* bank

Listen. You are not an escort service. You are not paying this person to show you a good time, or to make you feel important. They are not paying you to feel loved or important. You are not trying to show them that you are no longer the ninth grade freak who couldn't get a date to the dance.

Just because you're so concerned that this person won't take the job, you pant wildly and slobber all over the dog. The dog's thinking, "Man, I didn't even have to sit, or shake, or speak. I didn't even wag my tail and this one here's already giving me the 'what-a-cute-puppy look!'" Woof! Woof!

1. THE ROUGH VERSION

On the contrary, one way to audition the candidate's bonding and rapport skills is to start out the audition a little bit rough, not "Ruff!" You know that you can bond and rapport with people because you're a nice person, but how is this sales candidate going to handle meeting a prospect? How about some SOB prospect who loves to bite and chew on salespeople? You know, the real pit bull type of prospect we all love so much. Keep telling yourself you are doing this because you know they are going to get slaughtered in the field. If it hurts them now, it's going to kill them later. Personally, I'd rather hurt someone than kill them.

Think about how your prospects are going to treat that candidate. Would your prospect treat your candidate by inviting them in, have them sit down, have a cup of coffee with them, ask about family and friends and history? Or would your prospect look at your salesperson and say, "What have you got? Why are you here? Stop wastin' my bleepin' time!"

Begin the audition the same way your prospect will treat that salesperson in real life and you will find some interesting reactions. The reason you do this is to see how this particular salesperson handles bonding and rapport.

TIPS

Treat the candidate the way a prospect would treat them to see how they are going to interact. After five or six minutes of this, you can let your guard down and let them know, "I was just testing you to see how you would handle a real prospect."

Hold your horses, though. Don't let your guard down for the interview, just for this type of "behavior" within the interview. If you relax too much, you're right back where you started. They'll own you.

2. THE COLD-CALL AUDITION

One of my favorites is the Cold-Call Audition. For example, let's say that your behavior would require a lot of pure, pure cold-calling. During the audition, you should be able to slide the phone across the table to the candidate and say, "Okay, here's a list of twenty names. Go ahead and cold-call." And watch them work! This is not sadistic. This is well within reason and practical.

Remember: you are not looking for great success here. You are looking for smooth technique, fearless attitude, creativity, and the ability to make a cold call without hesitation. This is the ultimate test to smoke out a salesperson that says they're a great cold-caller. If they really are great they will pick up the phone and start dialing for dollars. Even if they don't sell, it at least shows they have no fear, hesitations or reservations.

3. NETWORKS

The same move can be done if the behavior calls for a lot of networking with existing relationships. In the interview, there is no way to be sure they have the contacts and relationships you require in the BASE model. They may say it, but we all know how to tell when a salesperson is lying (their lips are moving). To make sure the salesperson is telling the truth, slide the phone across the table and ask them to set up two lunch meetings with existing people that fit the profile for which you are looking to sell. If they have the networked contacts this will be a no-brainer. If not you will know now that they have *sold you* all along and you just found a reason to take another dog to the shed and save yourself some time and money. Chick-chick...Blam!

4. SHOPPING SPREE

Speaking of money, one of my favorite ways to audition the candidate is in the area of money. If you tested them in the interview and have a belief that they have a high degree of comfort talking about money, it is now time to put them through the audition. Jump in the car with the candidate and take them to an electronics store. What salesperson does not like to go buy a new big-screen TV? When you get to the store, tell them you want them to help you pick out a new TV for your entertainment room. Let them know that you know nothing about TVs and you want their help.

Now it is time to watch them. See if they look at all the models or just look for the best one on the shelf. Do they look for the deal? Do they look for the lowest price? Right smack in the middle of the trip, I ask the candidate to show me how much money they have in their pocket. Sounds like a lot of work to do all of this crazy stuff, right?

Think about this for a minute. By taking a simple trip down the street, I can learn the following things about this candidate:

1. I can learn their decision process by how many TVs they look at or test out.
2. I can learn if they'll ever ask a prospect to buy a TV if they ask me to buy the TV.
3. I can learn their questioning skills based on the questions they asked me about the TV.
4. I can learn their comfort level with money based on how much money they carry around and the way they respond.

There is so much to learn by inserting this simple step into the audition. This is reality, something they are going to be faced with every day. It sounds hard-ass and over-the-top, but I don't think you see any doctors out there who are allowed to operate without showing a few skills beforehand. They are trusted with a customer's pain and so are your salespeople. You have the specific right to do what you need to do in order to get what you want and deserve. They have the right to walk out the door with no harm done. You think I'm crazy? "You may be wrong but you may be right. Owu-owu." Enter guitar lick. Save the sax solo for when you hire them.

5. THE CANDIDATE'S SOCIAL ENVIRONMENT

The audition should be a fun part of the process. This gives you not only a time to put the final notches in the decision but to also see the candidate in a social environment. Take the candidate to lunch on the way to the electronics store. Get to know them and make sure you can work with them.

A friend of mine dated a guy in college. I swore she loved him, but the poor guy had an eating problem. It was like an episode out of the *Seinfeld* show. He wasn't a binge eater or a carnivore to her vegetarianism. He just ate with his mouth wide open about every fourth chew. She could see the potatoes rolling around in his big open cavity. Maybe that would be all right, but broccoli? I'm not saying you can't decide not to hire a person because of the way they eat, but think of how your client will see this person if they ever dined together. If you feel they are socially acceptable, and every other aspect of this search matches, then you eventually may hire them.

CHAPTER 9
MAKE THE OFFER

CHAPTER 9
MAKE THE OFFER

N ow you are almost there. You have completed eight of the ten steps required for a successful hire. You designed your ideal candidate, you did a phone interview, you tested, you interviewed, and you auditioned. Now it is time to make the offer. Don't blow it here. If you have ever been to the zoo, you would know just how much it takes to feed a tiger.

Tigers eat a lot. They don't eat hamburger. They like good quality meat and lots of it. If you feed a horse they only eat straw, but due to the quantity, their food can still add up to a lot of money. Not as much as the fresh meat for a tiger, but still some good cash. The same applies to a salesperson. The only cheap animal to feed is a dog. Mash up a bunch of chicken parts and wheat, or something, and they'll eat it. They'd eat your shoe if you'd let them.

The universal rule applies to a salesperson's comp plan: "You will get what you pay for." I like to say, "If you pay with peanuts you will get monkeys." I want to make one thing perfectly clear: if you are not willing to pay for the talent, you will not get it. Warning. The following is a bullshit meter:

1. I want a person who is hungry.
2. I want the salesperson that will work on commission and make their own destiny.
3. I want the self-starter who is willing to put the time in to get to the big bucks.

If you ever find yourself uttering this filthy dreck, please stop kidding your ridiculously disillusioned jackass self and pinch the most thinned-skin part of your mongrel body. Would you work for free? No! So don't expect a professional to do the same. This isn't the medieval times, with class systems and serfdoms. First of all, what you just asked for (see: "practically begged") is a desperate, disorganized, untrained, undisciplined pushover who fits at least one of the following scenarios:

a. Fresh out of college
b. Hiding a past felony conviction
c. A lateral mover
d. Currently on unemployment
e. Recently fired
f. A has-been
g. A "soul searcher"
h. A "Team Player"
i. A Wendy Whiner

And the drum roll, please!

j. Your replacement

These are the only people who are going to get excited about the things I mentioned above. Yes, I know you want a tiger and the above statements "suggest" you want a tiger. However, they also strongly say, "I want a dog. I want a dog. I want a dog!" Save yourself the time and go to the pound and pick up your dog. Those dogs truly need you and will do *anything* to please you. That is, anything *but* sell, sell, sell! Otherwise, you're just telling a smart salesperson that you want to be a miser and hang on to all your money like a spoiled child while the dog drools beneath you, at your feet. And when the dog's been a good dog, maybe - just maybe - you'll throw the bitch a small scrap of bone.

If you ask for it, you are going to get it. Remember the ad I posted for you in Chapter 4, "Fill the Pool." What you ask for (you think you want) is what you are going to advertise for (what "they" think you want) and is what you are going to get (don't want!). Let me say it again. Great talent is expensive. Be prepared to pay for it. If you are saying any of the things I listed above, you have wasted your money on this book. You will not - I repeat - *will not* find top, talented salespeople who will work for cheap or for free.

Otherwise, you can take your show on the road to all the colleges in America, and sell Visa cards because that is the kind of salesperson you are looking for. The reason I say this is because selling Visa cards to college students is like handing out candy. Most of the credit card salespeople are fresh out of college anyway and most college students have no idea what credit is, more or less seeing it as "free money." Then they'll spend the next ten years of their life buying self-help books that help them get out of debt. If you want a green-faced hack, then hire one. But do not hire one because of anything you read in this book. Don't even mention my name in public, please.

Let me give you a great real world example. If you're looking for a top salesperson that already hits all of his sales goals and expects to make 100K at his current company, then you need to start looking for a salesperson that is at least making 80K. If they are not making 80K now, they will not work hard enough to make 100K for you. The salesperson making 50K now will stop when he hits 80K and, therefore, will not do enough to get to 100K and will never be a top performer for you. If the candidate is making 80K now, he is probably spending 85K. There is no way he can live on a 30K base and wait for commission to come in later. He will starve after about 30 days at that pay rate. When you have found the right talent it is time to step up to the plate and pay for it.

DETERMINING COMP PLANS

Here is how to decide what to offer a candidate. First, start out by deciding how much revenue a top salesperson will produce. Think this through carefully. Have conviction about it. Next, ask yourself this important question: "What is the *most* I would be willing to pay to get that revenue generated by a salesperson?" Whatever that number equals, be prepared to ask a second question: "Would I pay 5% more or would that be too much?" Get the *highest* amount that you would pay to get that revenue. This is what you offer to your sales candidate.

With this offer you will know there will be no negotiations, and no waiting. It is the very best you can do. If they ask for more you have no hesitation and you can say "no." There are lots of places to shop around, bargain-hunt or negotiate. This is not one of those places. Pay for the talent. Enough said. You know the candidate you want. You know what you are willing to pay for the talent.

Background Check

1. References: Who Do You Skip?

Just before you make the offer it is time to do a background check. There are a few "do's" and "do not's" with this step. The first major "don't" is to call the references they give you. Are you stupid or just lazy? Even Uncle Rocky can check their current references. In reality, what idiot is going to list a reference that will truthfully tell you something bad about the prospective hire? If I could check the family tree on every person who applied with me, I would, because there's something called a "married" name. Hell, my editor has three sisters, all married. His three sisters could actually be his top three references, and they'd all have three different last names than him. How do you check for that?

If the candidate got this far you know they are a good salesperson. What are you thinking by calling the references they give you? Of course their reference is going to say, "Oh Jimmy is the greatest salesperson I have ever had work for me. If I could hire him back I would in a heartbeat." Listen. If they wanted to hire him back they never would have let him leave. Or, it just may be that the person that let him go is (read: "needs to be") sitting in bed right now, reading this book because they need to hire a great salesperson.

Obviously, there is a time when a competitor bucks up and makes someone an offer they can't refuse, but I truly believe there is always a way to counter that and still bring in the revenue required to pay for it in the end. You should never lose a candidate because they are too good. Just remember that money isn't everything and there are many creative ways to keep someone at your company. Three books from now, perhaps I'll address that one, but you should do some research now and create a few options of your own. Maybe then you can write a book!

2. References: Who to Call

So if you can't call the references they give you, whom do you call?

Remember this: *call the references they <u>don't</u> give you.*

Start with the past customers they used to sell or service. Call these customers and find out if they liked the sales rep. Dig in deep. Make sure they liked the sales rep, and that they liked them for all the right reasons. Some salespeople tend to give away the farm to their customers. Some do this legally and some do it illegally. Customers like to get the farm for free, especially when there's no rooster to wake them up and ruffle their feathers.

Make sure this particular reference likes and respects the salesperson for the right reasons - the same things you look for in your perfect hire. Technically, you are looking to see if the reference is matching the salesperson's BASE with yours. You have to remember that they don't know what BASE is, but you can ask them questions to determine their knowledge of the candidate's BASE, regardless. Think: the candidate didn't know what BASE was either (and wasn't aware of its existence), but you determined their BASE by the questions you chose to ask them. When calling on the reference, this just means you will have to revise the questions you asked the candidate throughout the interview process and cater them to the reference. You'll get the BASE from the reference just the same. It's that simple.

3. THIRD-PARTY CHECKS

Aside from checking references, you also can do some standard background checks. The most efficient way to do background checks is to trust the experts. There are third-party sources that you can hire to do the background check for you. They can range from drug testing to DMV screens, to criminal and credit checks. Just remember that whatever you find will be judged on your terms. You can ask the candidate to explain themselves so you may make your own reasonable decision, or you can drop them.

CHAPTER 10
SUCCESS
CONDITIONING

SUCCESS CONDITIONING

S o you think it is all over, right? If you think it is over, you have another thing coming (insert bone-crunching guitar). Maybe this is why you've experienced so much turnover in the past. You think the hiring process is done after you hire the salesperson. While just hiring a great person may be enough in other positions, it is not enough for the salesperson. You need to condition the salesperson for success once they get hired. This process should last about 90 days. When you are done with that 90-day period, only then will you have a great salesperson. If you skip this step, you will lose the effectiveness of this whole process. You should know by now that this means everything you have done thus far.

FIRST 90 DAYS

From the time the candidate accepts the offer to the time they start, it is your task to make a plan. Nobody knows your business better than you. No matter how good a salesperson is, they will not know more about your business than you on their first day. You need to make a detailed plan for the first 90 days of the salesperson's employment. This plan must be infinitely detailed and it must be in writing. Nothing is too small to be left out of this 90-day plan.

1. FIRST DAY/FIRST WEEK

The first part of the plan must be a detailed first week. Start out with the first day. Break down the first day into an 8-hour plan. It is critical to start the salesperson out right, and this first eight hours is their first-impression. The first day and week should be explicit in what you expect. This week should get the salesperson acclimated to the environment. Get the e-mail in place, get the phone set up, explain the benefits, etc. Have the business cards on the salesperson's desk when they walk in and have all the important people that they need to meet come to *them*. Have every minute of the first week booked and laid out so that the new hire feels the first week is not a whirlwind. Think of all the "basics" that may get in the way later, and get them solved.

I once worked for a place that had me work the first day, without e-mail. They sat me down in front of a crappy computer, gave me a broken earpiece for an outdated phone, and had me meet with a dandruff-littered man who laughed when I asked him about business cards. Granted, temp jobs are always a bitch on the first day, but does it really have to be so tough? Seriously folks, this is your first, and maybe last impression. And while we're at it, enough of the hazing crap that so many companies still accept. Public relations and advertising firms are notorious for it. Make the new person feel like dirt to gain their respect, right? Wrong! So many people find it acceptable to fall into the old, "Hey! That's what they did to me" garbage. Give them your integrity and respect, not the opposite. Think of the details and treat this person with true respect and they will be well on their way to having everything they need to succeed.

2. FIRST 30 DAYS

After the first week-plan, look at the first 30 days. How many meetings do you expect? How many calls do you expect? How many proposals? And how long should it take them to get up to speed, per se? Make a spreadsheet and map in exact detail the behaviors and results you expect. Is this a tedious exercise? *Yes.* Should you expect the salesperson to do this? *No.* You are the leader, now go ahead and lead. If you can't do this, then hire someone to do it for you. Most of all, do not expect the salesperson to walk in on their first day and know exactly what they need to do to be successful. Lead by leading, and lead by *avoiding*.

 A pitfall you must avoid is to have the new salesperson ride with your experienced veteran. "Go ride with Big Bill and you will learn how to sell." That's a death trap, not a plan.

If I could have patented that one, I wouldn't be writing this book. I'd be drinking Mai Tai's in Argentina with your first hire, dying my hair, though for completely different reasons. All week long the only things the new salesperson is going to learn are Big Bill's bad habits. Some of my favorites are how to avoid the boss, how to do as little as possible to get by, and how to cook your numbers.

Don't let your existing people train your new ones. Be a leader and train them yourself. You're the one who's done all the work to find the great salesperson, so why blow it here? If you don't have the ability to train, then you must find a professional trainer that can understand the process you have set up. They must understand your candidate BASE, your company BASE and your comp plan, or their training will be useless. You also should sit through the training itself to ensure the trainer is living up to their end of the bargain. If not, you should either "redirect" the trainer or fire their ass. You'll know when you have a good trainer because you are used to sniffing out dogs by now, and a bad trainer should find themselves barking up the wrong tree... yours!

There is an important distinction we should make at this point regarding training. You should *not* be training your new hire *how* to sell. You should *not* be training your new hire how to sell *more*. You should be training them how you want them to sell your product or solution. They should be learning your reporting systems and/or tools. They should be learning your company policies and procedures. They should be getting to know your current customer base. They should be getting to know their peers and your company management. If they are learning how to sell, you have not learned a single thing and you must buck up and either start over or fire yourself. And for the record, I highly doubt that anyone, from the advice of this or any other book, is going to fire himself or herself.

3. 60 DAYS AND BEYOND

The same plan must be made for the first 60 days and the first 90 days. The salesperson needs to know exactly what you expect from them and when the plan is made you need to share it. Review it with the salesperson and make sure they completely agree and accept everything. Every little detail. If the salesperson knows what is expected of them, they will know what to do and there will be no disappointments later on from either you or the salesperson. This is your best way to avoid marriage counseling later on. This is the moment you've been waiting for. No "She said, he said." Write it down, verbalize it, shake on it, and let it fly. You may now kiss the bride.

CHAPTER 11
LET'S GO SELL

CHAPTER 11
LET'S GO SELL

You are done. You've hired a superstar. Now you can fly to Argentina, sit back, dye your hair, relax, and drink margaritas by the pool. Just make sure you have your accountant nearby, because the money is going to start flowing faster than my Uncle Rocky can replace the gumballs in the local Buenos Aires supermarket gumball machine. Will this make you successful? Will this make you happy? That is for you to determine, but you now know that you have worked that much harder to avoid the illusion and become the illusionist. You too can "make it look easy."

It goes without saying that there is more to running a business than just hiring great salespeople. In my entirely subjective and biased opinion, however, the single most important group of people in your company is always going to be your salespeople. As the person responsible for hiring, that might indeed make you *the* most important person in your company. Those salespeople will single-handedly determine whether or not you and your company are a success or a failure. Lately, we hear a lot about CEOs, accountants, or board members that bring their company to ruin. Don't think that bad salespeople can't do the same.

Like the ancient ruins of old and great civilizations, people will loot your company for gold or wield a machete, pick or shovel to find interesting artifacts that can serve their own selfish interests. A failed or failing company is ripe for invasion, whether that failure is due to the worms from within, or the ships outside your seaside fort. An honest, hard-working sales team is like good, pressure-treated wood. It can fortify your walls and has the most influence on the outcome of your organization. It is for this reason that you should put that much more effort into hiring only the best salespeople for your company. Anything less means you expect and accept the worst, even if it is in that dark, cavernous hole where our "denial" resides and hides: the shadow.

A very wise business philosopher once said, "Sales fix most business problems." This is entirely true. If you have enough revenue, most of your business problems are easier to fix. Just pick up any business magazine today and you can't help but read about the CEOs of huge companies that have done everything legal and illegal to boost the all-powerful revenue numbers in an effort to inflate their worth. The only thing they didn't do was put a true focus on hiring great salespeople.

Remember: real growth is new business, not cooking the old books and calling it new stew! Good salespeople are the most effective ingredient. Don't get caught being a chef with his pants down, holding two steaming pots.

In business you either grow or die. There are only two ways to grow: you either acquire other companies and get their revenue (looting, artifacts) or you go out and sell more of the stuff you already have. If you have the best salespeople on your team you will ultimately grow your revenue and succeed in business. I know my views are biased and skewed, but I have an intense respect and admiration for anyone strong enough to get into the sales profession because of the pressure they endure. They are expected to help a company succeed...directly

It is for the true great salespeople that I wrote this book. It is for the companies that need to find these great salespeople that I wrote this book. I truly hope you will give great salespeople a great home where they can grow and succeed, rather than dwindle and burn out. Lastly, it is for you who have read thus far that I wrote this book. You are either a trooper with a self-deprecating sense of humor or an outright masochist. Either way, you took one step closer to achieving your goals and dreams, and that's always admirable in any profession.

If you made it through to this part of the book, you also have realized by now that I am not a world-class author. In any case, I have made a world-class pile of mistakes in the process of hiring great salespeople, and I too am always learning how to do a better job. Along the way my company, SalesKingdom, has perfected a process to hire and *retain* great salespeople.

If you follow this process, you too will be able to hire the best of the best and grow your company to success. Make it a company I would be happy and proud to work for, and one my mysterious, imaginary Uncle Rocky Spargaloogonoose would want nothing to do with, and you've already paid for this book in spades. And you'll never have to worry about selling gumballs to Moose Lodges. As always...

Good Luck and Good Selling

Joe's Secrets at a Glance

CHAPTER 1: COMING CLEAN

The author understood that in order to create and/or implement a process, we must understand who we are and what we truly want and need from the process. And, it is extremely necessary for the reader to understand the history, experience and intentions of the author. Because this is a professional self-help book, it is extremely important that the reader examine their personal and business perspective before implementing this process. This includes an examination of the product/service being sold, the current hiring practices, the current staff and administration, as well as the person who is most responsible for implementing this process, which should be the reader. At the very least, the reader should be prepared to make drastic change for the better that may seem difficult and laborious. The reader must uncover weakness and pitfalls and set the stage for an honest examination of the company and the self. Remember that individuals hire individuals, and we can only create and maintain a strong company by hiring the right individuals, especially in sales. We are highly subjective beings and must learn to become highly objective for much of this process.

CHAPTER 2: FILLING SOMEONE'S SHOES

The author's painful, often comical search for a better process may sound familiar to most readers, which should help them empathize/sympathize with the author's plight. Most salespeople are taught to uncover a prospect, customer or client's pain, which contributes to this process. Many mistakes were made before this process was proven, and will help the reader learn from them and avoid them. Mistakes are costly, resulting in unnecessary employee termination. This is traumatic to the individual and to the company. However, it is likely you will need to terminate one or several employees to gain a better fit for your company and to build a better team with no weak points. This difficult decision will save you from doing it again. Learn the analogy of tigers, horses and dogs inside and out. Understand the personalities that surround you, understand what you are looking for and be prepared to seek those personalities that make your company strong and successful.

CHAPTER 3: CREATE THE "BASE"

This is the first actual step in the process we call Eight Steps to Hiring a Tiger™. Ideally, you are looking to hire a tiger, which represents the most forward-thinking, pro-active, responsible individual you can hire for your company, regardless of the sales job you are filling: hunter, farmer or fisherman. Remember that a hunter seeks out business, a farmer farms it from the same or existing place (always trying to get more out of the same plot of land) and a fisherman puts out the hook and waits for something to bite. These three sales categories require great skills if you are to be the best and all three require some similar and perhaps some very different BASE requirements. The BASE (Behaviors, Attitudes, Skills Sets and Environment) not only helps you identify a hunter, farmer or fisherman, but also helps you find the perfect salesperson within those categories. This recruiting process absolutely cannot be implemented without starting with your BASE. In addition, this is your first chance to stay objective in the process, foregoing your own subjective opinions and biases for the more objective needs of the company. You must confront your pitfalls, including your fear of change, laziness and lack of confidence and/or your fear of facing major change. You must be looking and willing to eliminate your poor performers and commit to finding tigers. Your past is no longer relevant. Think of the present and future, using the BASE as your new guide.

CHAPTER 4: FILL THE POOL

Focus on building a 100+ candidate pool per hire (or three hires at most). Head hunting is complex and requires creativity, a proactive attitude and confidence. Think of all of the traditional and non-traditional ways you can fill your pool before you begin. You must not seem desperate, and are better off searching when you do not need candidates. Be wise and fill your pool before you dismiss an employee. Place ads where creative job seekers find jobs and always describe the candidate, not the position. Remember: if you show you are hungry, not desperate, you will attract tigers. Small candidate pools fuel desperation though a lack of choices. When contacting salespeople, understand and use the salesperson's mindset. If you try too hard to sell them, you may distract them with your poor sales skills, but enthusiasm, honesty and integrity will sell the position for you. The process should give you confidence. When possible, gain competent candidates through competent referrals, especially those from current clients.

CHAPTER 5: THE PHONE SCREEN

As another objective step in this process, the phone screen is efficient and doesn't require face-to-face time. It can be ten minutes or less and can be designed to elicit only "yes" or "no" answers, eliminating subjective or roundabout answers. It also keeps test parameters in the hands of the interviewer. Candidates can "sell to" the test or lie. This test uses your top ten BASE requirements (you should have at least 100 BASE requirements) and can be given by anyone in the company, requiring only intermediate phone skills. If a candidate is insulted by this stage of the process, eliminate them, as this and other character flaws should not be tolerated. Good salespeople will try to sell themselves. This stage eliminates that, but it can be noted if a salesperson is inquisitive and asks well-placed questions (selling). If they don't, they probably have poor listening skills. Someone other than the final decision maker must conduct this stage of the process. Otherwise, the decision maker may "lean" toward certain candidates due to early subjectivity.

CHAPTER 6: BE OBJECTIVE

At least forty people can move on to a third-party test, given by an outside party previously chosen by you and/or company management. This is yet another objective stage because your company is not giving the test. It is important to ensure, prior to accepting this third-party test, that you understand what qualities and objectives you want from this test and how it will illuminate the qualities of your perfect salesperson. It can give you an outside perspective with which you can work and determine who moves forward, but in the wrong hands it also may cloud your judgment, objectively and subjectively. It must make sense for you alone, and must be built on your BASE requirements. SalesKingdom recommends an all-encompassing test from PeopleAnswers. Avoid major pitfalls. Realize that salespeople can "fool" the test, or learn to score well on third-party objective tests. Remember: because someone "scores" well on a written test does not mean they can execute in real life. Candidates also can "cheat" for offsite tests by sharing passwords, etc. As one step in the process, it's a great tool to find your perfect salesperson when used in conjunction with all steps of the process.

CHAPTER 7: THE INTERVIEW

Designed for a minimum of ten to thirty clients, this step lasts about 45 minutes to an hour and helps cross-reference answers given in the prior, third-party objective tests to dig deep and rule out cheaters. Check for past behaviors that match your requirements and never "feed" answers. Get the candidate to explain rather than "confirm" their behaviors. Remember: good poker players never tip off their hand. A bad candidate will "yes" you to death, so fight your instinct to "like" people. Still remain objective but don't be afraid to start using your instincts. It is better to think someone is avoiding something or giving half answers than complete avoidance. Let them sell you and catch any inconsistencies on their résumé or otherwise. Avoid choosing people simply because they act, behave and/or look like you. Focus on behaviors with your mind on ethics, and remember this will "audition" next, where you'll witness behaviors in action. Pre-plan clearly defined grading criteria and do not deviate for someone you "like." All candidates should pass at least 65% of your criteria. If not, bring in a third party to monitor or test your decision. If you can objectively convince the third party, let the candidate move on. Remember: salespeople are not trees and you cannot "grow" them. They must be ready now, without training.

CHAPTER 8: THE AUDITION

In the audition, the candidate performs the behaviors and displays the attitudes and skills sets fit for your environment. This a tightrope: push the candidate to uncover their true attributes without overdoing it. By now, you're auditioning the cream of the crop and have a decent relationship. This makes it difficult to push ("hurt") the candidate, but you must be tough to test the candidate's bonding and rapport skills and overall resolve. Remember: If you hurt the candidate now, they are less likely to get slaughtered in the field. How will your prospects treat that candidate? Treat the candidate in the same manner and don't let your guard down. Relaxing brings you back where you started and a good salesperson will own you, which taints this process completely. Develop a clear plan for auditioning and be consistent with all candidates, even if you feel the candidate is failing from the start. Some salespeople can still pull it off in the end. Don't be sadistic but true-to-life, reasonable and practical. Look for smooth technique, fearless attitude, creativity, and the ability to act without hesitation. This test smokes out dogs using your newfound ability to do so. Have fun, keep it professional and uncover how they actually work. Doctors are entrusted with a patient's pain and so it is with your salespeople and your clients. Save your candidates, your clients and your company a lot of pain in the future.

CHAPTER 9: MAKING THE OFFER

Although you have undoubtedly made an impression on the candidate by now, this chapter highlights your first chance to make an impression on behalf of your company and how they perceive the candidate's value and, in general, their new hires. The old cliché rings true: you never get a second chance to make a first impression. You will need to use your BASE to develop your comp because BASE actually deals with a salesperson's money attitudes, which includes but is not limited to how much money they need to pay their bills, how much money their last company paid them, and how much money motivates them. At all costs, avoid appearing cheap or stingy. If you let a salesperson work for mostly or all commission only, you are asking for a desperate, disorganized, untrained, undisciplined pushover who doesn't value themselves and you will create an immediate sense of disrespect and distrust. In general, follow the 5/20 rule. If possible, give them 5% more than you want to give them, and make sure you do not offer them anything that is not within 20% of their current/former salary or comp. By treating this person with respect and paying them well, you are expected and entitled to check their background, thoroughly. This includes references they do not give you. This is your last chance to ensure you have done everything in your power to hire an ethical, trustworthy person. This makes this step every bit as important as the previous steps combined. The most efficient method for background checks is to trust the experts. Try to use an outside party for the background check, and if something seems inconsistent or your basic instincts tell something is wrong, judge things on your terms and ask the candidate to explain themselves so you may make your own reasonable decision, or drop them.

CHAPTER 10: SUCCESS CONDITIONING

Complete the process with integrity and class or completely drop the ball. This step, essentially, is the second half of your first impression. The hiring is not done after you hire the salesperson. They still need to be "conditioned," which includes the all-important first 90 days. Remember: you're not training them to be great salespeople, just an effective salesperson in your organization: acclimated to your environment, your protocol, etc. No salesperson knows your business better than you. You train or at least "acclimate" the salesperson. If not, you should closely monitor the person or people who do the training. Avoid letting the salesperson train with your other salespeople. They only pick up their bad habits. Plan the first eight hours, with no detail spared, including everything from e-mail to business cards. Have a salesperson start later than intended (with pay) if it helps you plan a perfect first day. Expectations are written down and in detail for the first 30, 60 and 90 days and even the first year, if possible. Review this plan together and sign it so you both clearly understand it and are satisfied with the terms. At all costs, don't allow corporate hazing and treat the new hire as an equal. Show you are a leader, command respect without resorting to belittling, and that you are aware of and in command of your office culture at all times and in all respects.

APPENDIX
Questions (requests for answers)

This is a list of questions we use to interview salespeople. Of course, we don't use all the questions on all the interviews but it certainly is a comprehensive list of questions to ask salespeople so you may dig deeper in the interview process.

1. Tell me some things about yourself so that I can get to know you better.
2. Do you have any goals or aspirations?
3. In what environments do you work best?
4. What managers have you reported to in the past and what responsibilities were attributed to their position?
5. If you were your former employer, how would you describe your greatest accomplishments to me?
6. What weaknesses would you need to overcome in order to be more competent in your current or past positions?
7. How do you think your former co-workers might describe you?
8. We understand it is taboo to not speak highly of your current employer. If you were allowed to speak freely, what suggestions would you offer that might improve this company?
9. If you've managed others, how do you assist poor performers?
10. Please describe your best employee.
11. When your company encounters a crisis situation, do you ask for help, or are you more likely to employ a go-it-alone solution?
12. If you were to offer solutions to your current company's problems, what might you say that would adversely affect your ability to seek new employment?
13. How do you monitor your goals, and is it different from how you monitor prospects?
14. Where are you looking to be regarding salary? *(They should answer, quickly. If not, this may show a money weakness.)*
15. Why did you leave your most recent employer? *(Listen for excuses. This demonstrates his/her propensity to offer excuses for poor performance.)*

16. Have you ever felt discouraged or frustrated, had personal problems, personality clashes, or demonstrated resentment or anger toward any one at a prior job? Example: what's the hardest thing you ever had to go through, personally?
17. How would you describe your leadership philosophy and style?
18. Describe your ability to learn things quickly.
19. Describe a complex situation in which you had to learn a lot in a short period of time.
20. How did you go about learning and how successful were the out comes?
21. Describe your skills regarding problem analysis.
22. Do people generally regard you as one who diligently pursues every detail, or do you tend to exhibit more of a broad-stroke approach?
23. Give me an example of a time where you dug for facts more deeply than what was expected from you.
24. Describe your decision-making approach when you are faced with purchase situations.
25. Are you decisive and quick or are you more thorough?
26. Are you intuitive, or do you work purely with the facts?
27. Do you involve many or few people in your decisions?
28. What are some of the most difficult decisions that you have made recently?
29. What are some of the best decisions that you have made in the past year?
30. Are you more comfortable dealing with concrete, tangible, short-term issues, or with more abstract issues?
31. How creative do you consider yourself?
32.. Are you better at planning the mission or executing the mission?
33. What are the biggest risks you have taken?
34. Which risks did not work well?
35. How will past customers rate and describe your technical expertise?
36. Are you truly on the leading edge, or do you fall a bit short in some areas?
37. How computer literate are you?
38. How well do you network in the community?
39. What seminars or formal education have you participated in, and when?
40. Looking back in your career, what were your most and least successful jobs?
41. Describe a situation in which the pressures to compromise your integrity were the strongest you ever encountered.

42. Describe a situation where you have confronted unethical people or decisions and chose not to say anything to avoid "rocking the boat."

43. Under what circumstances have you found it justifiable to break a confidence? A policy? A law?

44. Should you join our organization, what actions would you take during the first weeks?

45. What kinds of obstacles have you faced in your present or most recent job, and how did you handle them?

46. Give some examples in which you were expected to do a certain task, and on your own, went beyond the call of duty?

47. Who have been your major career influences and why?

48. How organized are you and by what standard do you judge organization?

49. What do you do to remain organized and what, if anything, do you feel you ought to do to be better organized?

50. When was the last time you missed a quota or goal?

51. Do you prefer large volumes of clients and meetings or a few focused clients to work with?

52. What makes you procrastinate?

53. Describe your work habits.

54. Describe a situation that did not go as well as planned. What would you have done differently?

55. Do you believe in asking for forgiveness rather than permission, or are you inclined to be sure your bosses are in full agreement before you act?

56. How much supervision do you want or need?

57. How do you alleviate stress?

58. How would I know that you are "stressed out"?

59. Describe yourself in terms of emotional control. What sorts of things irritate you the most or get you down?

60. How many times have you lost your cool in the past couple of months? *(get specifics!)*

61. Describe a situation in which you were the angriest you have been in years.

62. How much feedback do you like to get from people you report to, and in what form *(written, face to face)*?

63. What are the biggest mistakes that you've made in the past ten years, and what have you learned from them?

64. What are your principal developmental needs and what are your plans to satisfy them?

65. What have been the most difficult criticisms for you to accept?

66. How has your selling system changed over the years?
67. When were you so frustrated you did not treat a prospect with respect?
68. Do you have a sense of humor?
69. Tell me about a situation in which you were expected to work with a person you disliked.
70. Are you familiar with the term "active listening"?
71. How would you define it?
72. What would your customers say regarding how often and how effectively you use active listening?
73. How would you describe your level of assertiveness?
74. When there is a difference of opinion, do you tend to confront people directly, indirectly, or tend to let the situation resolve itself *(again, get specifics!)*?
75. Please give a couple of recent specific examples in which you were highly assertive, one in which the outcome was favorable, and one where it wasn't.
76. How would you rate yourself as a public speaker?
77. If I had a videotape of your most recent presentation, what would I see?
78. Describe the last time you "put your foot in your mouth."
79. How do you communicate with your organization?
80. How would you describe your writing style in comparison to others'?
81. Describe a couple of the most difficult, challenging, or frustrating prospects that you had to work with.
82. When you are in a slump, whom do you blame?
83. Please give a couple of examples of the most difficult political situations in which you have been involved, both internally and with clients.
84. Describe situations in which your negotiation skills proved effective and ineffective.
85. Describe a situation in which you were most effective at selling an idea or yourself.
86. What are the most important things that a sales manager can do for you?
87. How often do you attend some sort of training?
88. How do you go about establishing goals for performance?
89. How do you communicate your expectations to subordinates?
90. Do you consider yourself a "hands on" manager?
91. Describe your performance management system.
92. How effective have your methods been regarding follow-up on dele-

gated assignments?

93. Tell me about accountability.
94. How do you hold yourself accountable?
95. What happens when you don't achieve your goals?
96. Do you have goals in writing?
97. Let me see your written goals.
98. How do you track your goal progress?
99. Where do you see yourself in ten years?
100. How are you going to get there?
101. Do you naturally take control of the sale or do you have to think about it?
102. Tell me about a situation where you had to take control of the sales process.
103. Describe a situation where you had to sell as a team.
104. Describe situations in which you prevented or resolved conflicts.
105. How many hours per week do you work?
106. What are some of the things that motivate you?
107. How would you rate yourself regarding enthusiasm and charisma? Why?
108. Describe the pace at which you work.
109. How satisfied are you with your balance in life?
110. What are examples of the biggest challenges you have faced and overcome?
111. What level of urgency do you have?
112. Do you have any questions?

INDEX

30, 60, & 90-day plan, 83, 115-117, 130
  as research project, 91, 93-94
ads, 108
  placement of, 50-51, 126-127
  writing of, 51-52
appointments, 30, 39, 64, 83
arrogance, 69
assessment tests, 67, 127-128
  aptitude, 74
  behavioral, 75
  cheating on, 78
  PeopleAnswers, 76-78
  psychological profiles, 73-74
attitudes, 90, 99, 128
  about money, 32-33, 48, 84
  decision making, 33-34, 84
  emotional discipline, 37-38, 86
  goal setting, 38
  in BASE, 28, 32-36
  need for approval, 34-36, 39, 85
auditions, 54, 94, 99-103, 128-129
BASE, 25-42, 43, 76, 94, 99, 102
  acronym for, 28, 126
  compensation and, 129
  head hunting and, 52
  interviews and, 95, 127-128
  phone screen and, 63, 67, 127
  references and, 111
  training and, 117
  writing ads and, 51
behaviors, 41, 51, 99, 101, 128
  first 30 & 60 days, 116-117
  in BASE, 28-31, 32
  tests for, 75, 82-83, 90
  typical in sales, 29-30
candidate pool, 47-49, 63, 73, 75, 126-127
  head hunting and, 52-53
  methods of building, 50-58
change, 5, 27, 36
  fear of, 28, 32, 63, 126
cold-calling, 30, 38, 64, 74, 86
  definition of, 29
  during audition, 101-102
commissions. See comp plans
comp plans, 18, 20, 26, 41-42, 91, 107-109
confidence, 39, 126
  in recruitment process, 25, 48
customer service
  as phone screening agent, 67-68
decision making, 132
  attitudes about, 33-34, 84-85
desperation, 47, 48, 53-54, 126-127
discipline, 37-38, 86
dogs, 15, 31-32, 51, 74, 76, 82, 86, 102, 117,
126
  audition and, 99-100, 129
  comp plans for, 107, 108
  desperation and, 47
  money and, 84
  need for approval, 16-17, 35-36
  recruiters and, 17-18
emotions, 28, 37, 39, 86-87, 133
employees
  complaints of, 89
  ethics of, 82
  management and, 35-36
  performance of, 26
  poor morale, 26
  retention of, 26
  rogue/unmanageable, 26
environments, 40-42, 77-78, 91, 99, 128, 131
  in BASE, 28, 126
  social, 103
  testing for, 64, 87-89
ethics, v, 35, 56, 128, 133
  candidate's, 69, 81-82, 129, 133
farmers, 38-39, 126
fear, 47
  of change, 28, 32, 63, 126
  of conflict, 36
  of rejection, 36-37, 85, 93
fishermen, 38-39, 126
gambles
  failure and, 19-20
  vs. risks, 5
gatherers, 49
giving, vi, 5-6
Glengarry Glenn Ross, 82
goals, vi, 38, 39, 90, 122, 131, 133-135
greed, 63
  decision making and, 8, 32
  victims of, 5
happiness, 4-5, 121
head hunting, 21, 52-57, 92, 93
  approaching candidates, 57
  candidate pools and, 52-53, 58, 126
  ethics of, 56
  problems of, 17
  role-playing, 55-56
  success in, 17
honesty, v, 6, 69, 78, 87, 125, 127
horses, 15-16, 19, 35, 36, 82, 83, 126
  comp plans for, 107
  in auditions, 99
hunters, 38-39, 126
interviews, 63-69, 81-95
  dogs and, 17
  mistakes during, 100

objectivity and, 65, 68, 127-128
past example, 90
sample questions for, 131-135
introductions
definition of, 30
Jung, Carl, 8, 34, 36
leads, 91
definition of, 29-30
listening, v, 3, 39, 127, 134
loglines 13-14, 15
Magic Kingdom, The, 89
management, 6, 8, 35, 37, 76, 87-88
lack of vision, 26
scapegoats and, 7
styles of, 9, 20, 40, 42, 76, 95, 134
marketing
company survival and, 9
meetings, 31, 41, 83, 90, 116, 133
Meyers Briggs, 73
mistakes, 7, 125-126
company survival and, 8-9
during interviews, 100
in recruitment process, 25, 35, 40
learning from, 3, 4, 8, 26-27, 29, 122,
133
successes and, 5
money, vi, 27, 108, 110, 121
attitudes about, 8, 32-33, 39, 64, 84, 102,
129, 131
happiness and, 4-5
networking, 29, 58, 59, 102, 132
objectivity, 43, 85, 125, 126, 128
3rd party tests and, 70, 73-78, 81
during phone screen, 65, 66, 68, 127
references and, 92
patience
during recruitment process, 27
in sales cycle, 38
PeopleAnswers, 76-77, 94, 95, 127-128
phone screen. See interviews
pitches
screenwriter's, 13-14
proposals, 31, 83
recruiters
dogs and, 17, 18
typical M.O., 18-19, 20
recruitment process
arrogance and, 69
common mistakes, 25
confidence and, 25, 48
desperation and, 47-48
ideal, 20
networking and, 59
patience during, 27

sentimentality in, 27-28
timing of, 49
references, 92, 110-111, 129
referrals, 30, 39
definition of, 30
to build candidate pool, 58-59, 127
rejection, 85, 91, 93
research projects, 92-94
résumés, 19, 65
risks, 132
vs. gambles, 5
role-playing, 55-56, 82, 94
SalesKingdom, 21-22, 49, 53-54, 68, 76, 92,
122, 127-128
salespeople
arrogance of, 69
companies and, 9, 121-122
desperation and, 54
income of, 4
kinds of, 15, 38-39
listening and, v
storytelling and, v-vi
training of, 83, 116-117, 128, 134
typical behaviors of, 29-30
screenwriters, 13-14
self-knowledge, 7-8, 125
sentimentality
during recruitment process, 27-28
skills sets, 38-39, 91, 99, 128
checklist, 39
in BASE, 28
testing for, 87
success
giving and, 5-6
mistakes and, 5
Target Training International, 73
tigers, 15, 54, 82, 126
comp plans for, 107
definitions of, 17-18
in the audition, 99
references and, 92
self-reliance of, 16-17, 35
training, 83, 116-117, 128, 130, 134
professional, 117
typical example of, 27
usahire.com, 50
video, 4
weakness, 131
admitting, 6-7, 125

THIS BOOK DOESN'T STOP AT THE LAST PAGE!

We want to hear from you !

Join our email list to continue your experience.

WBusiness Book is not just a business book publisher, it's a community for business readers who learn and share their experiences.   Sign up for our mailing list at **ww.Wbusinessbooks.com** and join the WBusiness Community

WBusiness Books
an imprint of New Win Publishing
9682 Telstar Ave. STE. 110
El Monte, CA 91731
Tel: (626) 448-4422
Fax:(626) 602- 3817

W **Business**
    Books